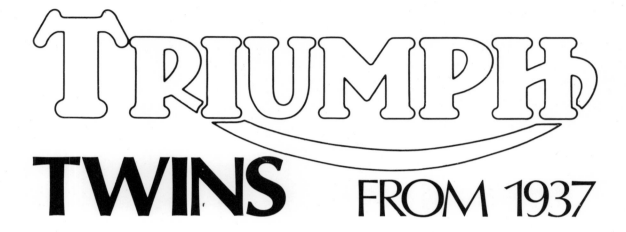

TWINS FROM 1937

Road Tests and Features from
The Motor Cycle & Motoring Cycling

Compiled and introduced by Cyril Ayton

BAY VIEW BOOKS

Published 1990 by
Bay View Books Ltd
13a Bridgeland Street
Bideford, Devon EX39 2QE

Reprinted 1991

ISBN 1 870979 17 6

Printed in Hong Kong

Contents

Introduction

The coming of the Triumph twin really did change the face of motorcycling. After Edward Turner blazed a trail in 1937 with his svelte yet practical design it was certain that other manufacturers would follow. The interval before the rival models appeared would have been briefer had the Second World War not occurred. By 1948, however, three years after the end of the war, all the other leading makers were producing vertical – more correctly "parallel" – twins.

The once-ubiquitous single was on its way to dodo-land. Years later, when Mr Honda took an interest in big motorcycles, with Europe and the USA in mind, he kicked off with parallel twins patterned, albeit with one or two significant variations, on the Triumph.

In the 1930s there was no sense of inevitability in the motorcycle world's advance towards multi-cylinders. On the contrary. Motorcyclists are in the main content with the contemporary condition of their chosen transport. In pre-Speed Twin times motorcycles typically had a single-cylinder engine. There were few complaints on that score. The single fulfilled all purposes. In humble small-capacity form it provided cheap and reliable everyday transport. For family use it was of 500 or 600cc, usually with side valves, heaving away at a heavy motorbike attached to a sidecar crowded with kids and mother. In a sports bike the single had overhead valves, sometimes with ohc operation, a high compression ratio and a high exhaust system. It made a lot of noise and gave an entirely adequate performance.

What *was* inevitable was Mr Edward Turner's decision to produce a multi-cylinder. In 1936 he had been appointed general manager and chief designer of the Triumph Engineering Company. He took over a range of ohv and sv singles plus a 650 ohv vertical twin designed some years earlier by Valentine Page and sold, in depressingly small number, for sidecar hauling.

Turner titivated the singles with extra chrome and fresh silver paint. He made interior improvements, with new cylinders and polished ports. The new bikes took the name "Tiger" – Turner had a gift for catchy motorbike names – and sold well. Page left Triumph for BSA. His 650 was dropped. Turner was unwilling to concede that the gentle, gifted Page had designed a viable motorcycle. He was – hard-headedly – correct in this, as he was in so many aspects of management, especially those touching on the all-important matter of assessing what would or would not sell. Here he was very shrewd: his acolytes, some critics even, said he had a touch of genius. It is clear that while he was dismissive of Page's efforts he was in no doubt that the concept of the twin-cylinder was the right one to pursue in a motorcycle world dominated by the single. Apart from

A 1959 649cc TR6 Trophy with die-cast light-alloy cylinder head, high-level siamesed exhaust system and large-section rear tyre

A batch of six special 500s was built by the Meriden factory for the 1966 Daytona 200-mile race in the USA. Buddy Elmore rode one to win; the following year Gary Nixon, similarly mounted, was successful

the intrinsic virtues of the design, marketing a successful twin would lift the Triumph company clear of the ruck and give it a special identity in the mind of the buying public.

Characteristically, he was at pains to hedge even such a carefully reasoned bet; also, he was familiar with the conservative ways of the motorcyclist. Thus the Speed Twin – and *there's* a memorable name – when it appeared in 1937 could have been mistaken for a comely single of the two-port type then in fashion. It was no bigger than a 500 single; indeed, it was fitted into the frame of the existing Tiger 90 500, with the standard forks and hubs and gearbox.

Incidentally, the designer's views on the twin (quoted by the authors of *The Story of Triumph Motor Cycles*) are as follows:

"A twin gives better torque. It will run at higher revolutions than a single of similar capacity without unduly stressing major components. Because the firing intervals are equal, which means even torque, the low-speed pulling is better. The engine gives faster acceleration, is more durable, is easier to silence and is better cooled. In every way it is a more agreeable engine to handle."

The late Bob Currie on a 1964 Bonneville. As midland editor of The Motor Cycle/ *later* Motor Cycle, *Bob was a regular caller at Triumph, Meriden. His duties included road-testing where his considerable bulk and weight tended to depress the performance of the lightweights turned out in bewildering profusion by the "two-stroke" factories in the Birmingham area. With a powerful machine such as the Bonneville, his skilful riding was shown to advantage. (Brave beyond the confines of the timing strip at MIRA, Bob Currie deserves posthumous recognition as the first motorcycle journalist to refer to Triumph's managing director simply as "Edward" in a published article)*

Close-up of the sand-cast light-alloy barrel and head of the 1948 Grand Prix racer. Derived from a stationary generator unit, the engine featured parallel porting. Ernie Lyons rode a GP to win the 1946 IoM Senior Manx Grand Prix, a feat repeated two years later by Don Crossley. The Grand Prix enjoyed mixed fortunes during its two-year production career, from 1948 to 1950, in the hands of a variety of leading riders. Often a match in speed for the other main senior-class racer of the day, the Manx Norton, it was not blessed with comparable reliability.

Why hadn't other manufacturers appreciated these evident truths? They had; but were happy to let Turner chance his – and his boss, J.Y. Sangster's – arm. Triumph might have come an expensive cropper. But the Speed Twin was a success from the beginning. It was extremely handsome. There was harmony – a balance – in the disposition, size and shape of the cylinder block, timing chest, gearbox and oil tank. On the nearside the large polished-alloy case for the primary chain took the eye. The fuel tank was, perhaps, a trifle ordinary in looks; mainly it was a matter of being a half-gallon too small, as was made clear when the speedier and even more eyeable Tiger 100, with a four-gallon tank, appeared in 1938.

And it was fast: 90mph was fast in 1937. The best sporting singles from Ariel and Norton, and Triumph's own Tiger 90, could crack 90. But their behaviour while doing so was different from the Speed Twin's. Singles pulled high gears, vibrated alarmingly and made an offensive (or entrancing?) noise: 80mph and over could be a serious business. In contrast, a Speed Twin would purr into the 80s. Vibration *was* present – it was, after all, a 360-degree twin – but was of a tolerable nature. This was a very civilised motorcycle. Only one other compared; but the 1000cc Ariel Square Four was much more expensive. (It will be recalled that this four-cylinder design originated with Edward Turner.)

Having designed in the Speed Twin a potential world-beater, Turner emerged from his drawing office ready to exploit the businessman side of his diverse personality. The twin evolved into several capacities and different applications over the years to become the lynchpin of Triumph production. Turner as super salesman, demanding managing director, calculating entrepreneur (careful with the pennies – wages – at home while entertaining dealers on a lavish scale in London and abroad) was fully a match for Turner the talented designer. There followed a period of sustained prosperity for the Triumph concern – and for E.T., as he was often known, in American tycoon style – that was unequalled in the history of the British motorcycle industry.

And *après nous le déluge*, E.T. might have said, finally. But probably did not for there is no record of a weakness on his part for snappy one-liners, borrowed or otherwise; the sentiment, however, suits his unretiring personality. He left Triumph in 1964, as the Japanese onslaught was gaining force, and died in 1974. He had warned the British industry of the threat posed by the Japanese. Nobody – and certainly not his own firm – altered course in any way to meet the threat. Perhaps he knew his countrymen too well. There is something fatalistic in his views, as summarised in an article appearing in *Motor Cycling* in late 1960: ". . . short of reshaping the British industry and methods as we have known them back to the days of Watt and Arkwright and beyond, it will be difficult for Britain to compete successfully with the Eastern problem. Japan secured a post-war flying start and has made the most of it". Other observers may have quarrelled with his view of Japan's "start"; but his comments on the scene nearer home must have been hard to fault.

Developments of the Speed Twin included 350s and 650s in various states of tune and – outside the scope of this book – a 750 in the 1970s. There were purpose-built racers. Ernie Lyons rode one to beat all the ohc Nortons in the first post-war race in the Isle of Man, in 1946. There were trials bikes and scramblers and even a world's speed record-holder. And as the pre-eminent maker of twin-cylinder motorcycles, Triumph were able to turn the clock back and made a case for the outdated side-valve as a suitable power unit for miltary bikes.

To return briefly to Mr Turner. He was the only man in the motorcycle industry who came near to being a public figure. Even now, were it possible to pose the question "Who designed the Triumph twin motorcycle?" to a company of middle-aged males the likelihood is that one or two would come up with the right answer. (Rather more would know that Issigonis was responsible for the Mini.)

With the man safely dead, commentators who had barely received a how-do-you-do from E.T. on their visits to Meriden were free to suggest a long-standing acquaintance that would enable them to speculate in a sometimes surprising way on the designer's life and work. His domineering ways and frequent outbursts had been common knowledge. In hindsight he was seen to have exhibited Napoleonic (or was it Churchillian?) tendencies. In this reading, it helped that he was of moderate height. It was known that he had not tolerated criticism of his designs. So: lack of maturity here? Warming to their theme, the amateur shrinks were able to acribe the Triumph motorcycle's less pleasing characteristics, such as its sometimes wayward handling, to guessed-at traumas in Mr Turner's childhood. Could long-ago tantrums really have been responsible for the ineffectual spring wheel, those under-damped forks, that ineluctable *scrunch* on bottom-gear engagement? In one published account, more judicious than others, Turner was pictured as an eight-year-old posturing in a grown-up's clothes. All very entertaining and, at the least, indicative of Edward Turner's crucial and sometimes controversial position in the British motorcycle hierarchy.

The following articles are taken from the two weekly magazines over a near-30 year period. In them the Triumph twin, in whatever guise or size, is given kid-glove treatment. It requires an alert, or intuitive, reader to identify any note of criticism. There are two reasons for the everything's-lovely-in-the-garden approach. One is that it was genuinely felt that the Triumph was a competent motorcycle deserving little adverse comment. The second is that the Triumph Engineering Co. was a major advertiser in the magazines. On reflection, it is possible that there was a third reason. The journalist and editor concerned in publishing any criticism would have had to face the wrath, on the telephone or face to face, of the forceful Mr Turner.

The magazines were seldom without a Triumph among their staff machines. At *The Motor Cycle* the assistant editor had one (and later another), as at different times had the technical editor and the trials/scrambles specialist. The technical editor was a much-lettered man with an appropriate interest in innovative engineering. On taking up his post at the magazine he indicated that he wanted a then-new lightweight flat-twin of advanced design as his staff machine. Wiser counsels – or, more likely, delays with the flat-twin, because of "teething" troubles, – led to substitution of a Speed Twin. From the management's point of view it is doubtful whether the Triumph was a good idea. It never gave trouble. The tech. ed. consequently found little to write about in connection with his new machine. Magazines have to be filled. Financially it's an advantage if most of the pages are taken up with the writings of in-house men. It's a safe bet that the flat-twin would have been troublesome, providing an inexhaustible source of cheap copy.

Motor Cycling's road-test editor of the 1950s covered many miles on a selection of the bigger twins. Another staff member raced a Tiger 100 in the Isle of Man.

Thunderbird for 1960 with new duplex-tube frame, forks and tank and 18in (in place of 19in) wheels. This was the year too when the Thunderbird (and the T110) received the rear "bathtub" treatment meted out previously to the 500cc models. The enclosure was not a popular success. It ranks as one of Edward Turner's few falls from grace in the styling area.

The Tiger 100 in 1948, with iron barrel and head. Note the tank-top instrument panel. This particular model is fitted with the rear spring wheel

By 1951 the Tiger 100, with headlamp nacelle, had a die-cast aluminium-alloy cylinder head and barrel with close-pitch finning. Power was up, to 32bhp. A dualseat had replaced the spring saddle, with consequent repositioning of the toolbox. The original fuel tank, with instruments, had been dropped in favour of a new style, having a parcel grid, in 1950.

Following the company's wins at Daytona, the name was adopted for a line of 490cc (69 x 65.5mm) unit-construction models.

NEW TRIUMPH DESCRIBED

An Interesting o.h.v. Vertical Twin Engine

BECAUSE it is well known that Mr. Edward Turner, managing director of the Triumph Engineering Co., Ltd., was the designer of that very ingenious and unconventional engine, the Ariel Square Four, it has been freely supposed that the new Triumph "multi" also would have four cylinders arranged in some novel but practical way. However, Mr. Turner, as those who know him well are quite aware, has anything but a single-track mind and in actual fact this interesting Triumph newcomer has two cylinders and a very simple general arrangement.

Nevertheless it does contain ingenious and unusual features and it would be highly inaccurate to think of this new model as simply a later and smaller edition of the old 650 c.c. twin. In fact none of the parts is the same as those of the earlier engine.

Compact and Light.

Up to a point it is true there is similarity. The two cylinders are vertical in one casting and the crankshaft lies across the machine. Moreover, both pistons rise and fall together. There the likeness ends.

The new engine is complete in itself and is not combined with a gearbox. It fits into a frame which is for most practical purposes the same as that of the Tiger "90" and, apart from the fact that the twin engine is a trifle lighter, the weight distribution of these two motorcycles is identical.

It has already been mentioned that the cylinders are vertical and are formed in a single casting. This is mounted on a crankcase of conventional style which is only slightly broader than that of a single. It carries on two bearings as usual a crankshaft which consists of three parts.

At the centre is a small flywheel with integral balance weights. Spigoted into each side of this is a piece which comprises a short shaft, a web, a crankpin and a circular flange which fits into the flywheel spigot and is held to it by bolts passing through the flywheel and the two flanges.

When assembled the two crankpins are in line, so that the firing intervals are evenly spaced. Because the two pistons move together and not in opposite directions, the balance is of precisely the same kind as a single. The forces involved, however, are somewhat smaller than in a single of the same capacity because the stroke is so much shorter.

Unusual Big-ends.

Actually the stroke is 80 mm. and the bores measure 63 mm., giving a total swept volume of 498 c.c. The compression ratio is about 7 to 1, a moderate figure for cylinders of this size, but the power developed is stated to be 29 b.h.p. at 6,000 r.p.m.

From what has been said of the crankshaft, students of design will have realized that rollers are not used for the big ends. Actually these are plain bearings, but not of quite the usual type. It should be explained that each connecting rod is an RR 56 Hiduminium forging. This material has excellent bearing qualities, but it lacks one feature of white metal. In an emergency such as the failure, temporary or otherwise, of the oil supply, white metal will fuse. This automatically provides additional clearance so that the bearing and shaft will not seize together to the détriment of both.

From these facts arises the big-end bearing design of this new Triumph twin. To take full advantage of the light Hiduminium rod it is arranged to bear directly on the steel crankpin. The bearing cap to complete the circle embracing the crank is, however, a steel forging lined with white metal. In this way the advantages of both metals are retained, together with a strong and rigid bearing cap.

No detailed description of the pistons is necessary because they are simple full-skirted affairs of well-tried type. Nor is there any novelty in the timing gear which consists of five wheels. A small one is mounted on the crankshaft and it drives an idler wheel above it. This in turn drives two half-speed gears arranged one on each side and slightly higher up.

The Cam Arrangement.

Each of these is mounted on a camshaft and the rear one meshes with the fifth gear which is attached to the shaft of a Lucas Magdyno placed behind the cylinders. Returning to the camshafts which are located one at the back and one at the front of the crankcase near its top, each shaft runs rather more than half-way across the engine and is mounted in two plain bearings.

On each shaft there are two cams very close together astride the centre line of the engine. The rear camshaft operates the inlet valves and the front one the exhausts, but the cam contours are identical in both cases and the two camshafts are interchangeable.

Immediately above each pair of cams is a phosphor-bronze block which carries

The new Triumph vertical twin is a remarkably good-looking machine. It has none of the bulkiness usually associated with "multis" and the engine actually weighs slightly less than a standard "90."

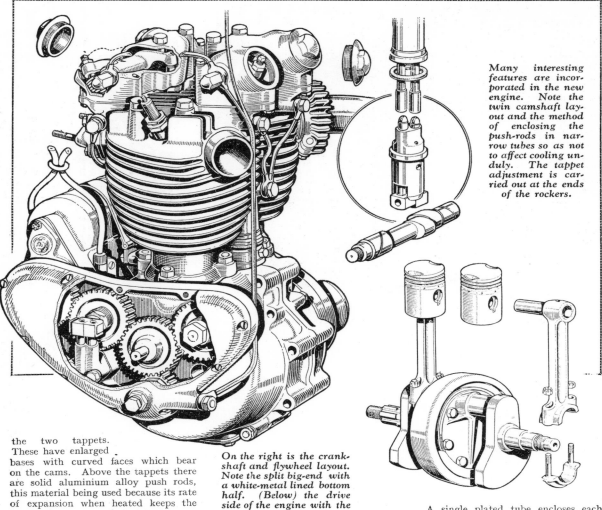

Many interesting features are incorporated in the new engine. Note the twin camshaft layout and the method of enclosing the push-rods in narrow tubes so as not to affect cooling unduly. The tappet adjustment is carried out at the ends of the rockers.

the two tappets. These have enlarged bases with curved faces which bear on the cams. Above the tappets there are solid aluminium alloy push rods, this material being used because its rate of expansion when heated keeps the tappet clearance nearly constant.

On the right is the crankshaft and flywheel layout. Note the split big-end with a white-metal lined bottom half. (Below) the drive side of the engine with the unit in the frame.

A single plated tube encloses each pair of tappets, and this tube is waisted or reduced in diameter for most of its length so that it causes very little obstruction to the flow of air between the cylinders which, although in one casting, are spaced sufficiently far apart to have fins between them.

The Valve-gear.

Each tube is provided with good oil-tight joints at both ends, and it need never be disturbed except when decarbonizing. Adjustment of tappet clearances is made at the push-rod end of each overhead rocker, there being a conventional lock-nut and set screw with a ball-end bearing in the cupped steel top of the push rod.

Both cylinder heads are formed in a single casting and the combustion spaces are hemispherical. The valves are arranged at a wide angle, the exhausts sloping forward, of course, and the inlets backward. Two light alloy castings mounted, one across the front and one across the back of the cylinder-head casting, enclose the valve stems and springs. They also carry the overhead rockers, and opposite each point of adjustment there is a screwed cap with a hexagon. The latter makes

The off side of the new Triumph twin unit. The two hexagon-headed caps give easy access to the valve tappet adjustment; below them will be noticed the pipes which drain surplus oil from the rocker box into the push-rod tube. Incidentally, how unusual is the appearance of an o.h.v. engine's timing side without push-rods.

A NEW TRIUMPH

(contd.)

it easy to tighten the cap so as to avoid oil leaks and, of course, removal of the cap makes tappet adjustment very simple.

Each cylinder has a single exhaust port from which a nicely curved pipe leads back to a cylindrical silencer by the chain stays, the appearance being very much that of an ordinary two-port engine. The inlet ports also are separate and are connected by a small Y-piece to a slightly down-draught Amal carburetter.

Lubrication.

Finally, so far as the engine is concerned, a word about the lubrication system. In the lower part of the timing case there is a double plunger pump of the usual Triumph pattern driven by an eccentric pin and sliding block. This pump is rather larger than its predecessor, and it delivers oil at a pressure of some 50 lb. per sq. inch.

Oil is fed to the big-end bearings through passages drilled in the crankshaft. A separate supply is taken by an external pipe to the two rocker boxes and is fed direct to the rocker bearings through the fixed spindles. The surplus is carried by short pipes into the push-rod tubes and thus lubricates the tappets and cams.

This interesting and very practical engine is mounted in a machine which in all other respects resembles the Triumph Tiger "90" 500 c.c. single. In spite of its extra exhaust pipe and silencer, the complete twin motorcycle weighs a trifle less than the single, but in other respects they are alike, and even in appearance the twin might easily be mistaken for a two-port single.

Solo gear ratios are 5.0, 6.0, 8.65 and 12.7 to 1, the sidecar ratios being 5.8, 6.95, 10.0 and 14.7 to 1. Both tyres are 26 ins. by 3.25 ins. The wheelbase measures 54 ins., and the overall length is 84 ins.

This is undoubtedly an interesting machine, but it is much more than that. From the earliest drawing-board stage trouble has been notably absent, we understand, and one of the experimental models with sidecar attached has covered 10,000 miles on the road in all weather and in a comparatively short time. Speeds of 90 m.p.h. solo are spoken of.

At an early date we shall publish a full road-test report, but already it seems clear that an outstanding machine has been added to the list of British motorcycles.

Petrol Cheaper.

Last Thursday morning motorcyclists filling up with petrol had a welcome surprise in the form of a ½d. per gallon reduction in price.

The Law Hinders "The Law."

Asked by a police constable to take him on the pillion seat to the scene of an accident on a little used country road, a Midland motorcyclist replied that he would go out of his way to help the law but . . . and drew the officer's attention to the L plates with which his machine was adorned. And, as the constable was not a "qualified driver," he had to walk nearly two miles.

"Torrens"

OF course, you have read the road test of the vertical twin Triumph on pages 610-612. I did not carry out the road test, but you can bet your bottom dollar that I took the opportunity of riding the machine—I always do when there is something interesting on test! My mileage was not colossal. It totalled just over one hundred, which was enough for me to know quite definitely that if the general run of production models is around the standard of the machine submitted for test this new vertical twin will cause a furore.

The day after the machine was returned to Coventry there was a trunk call. The man behind the design, the Triumph managing director, wanted to chat the model over. Could we suggest improvements?

Like you, I have read the road test. There is next to nothing I can add, or anyone else who rode the machine. As an idealist I might say, "I wish it had a spring frame," but taking the design as it stands, after riding the machine we had for test, what could I suggest? It has meant a very long think. About the only two detail points that have occurred to me are (1) the oil pressure gauge might be better illuminated for night work, and (2) the oil bleed for the rear chain is apt to throw lubricant where it is not wanted—over the rear of the machine.

The 497 c.c. "SPEED TWIN" TRIUMPH

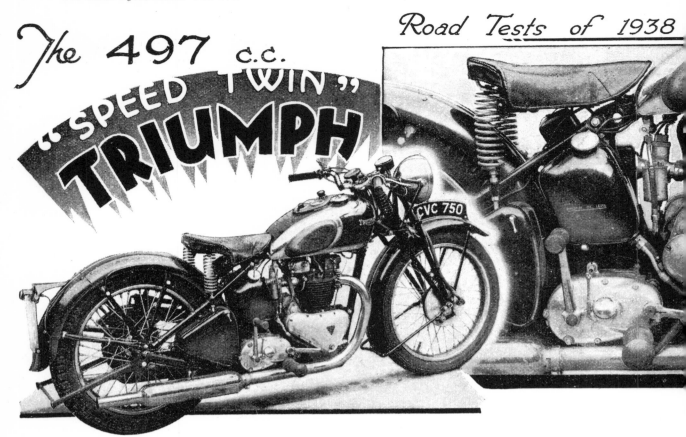

So compact and neat is the engine of the "Speed Twin" that the machine can easily be mistaken for a "single." The frame and other components are similar to those used for the single-cylinder Triumph mode's

The accessibility of the Triumph is clearly shown in this close-up of the engine. The neatly arranged oil leads and simple induction manifold are typical of the thoroughness of the design

NO one needs reminding that the new vertical-twin Triumph was one of the outstanding machines at the Earls Court Motor Cycle Show. Nor is it necessary to recapitulate the many interesting features of its design, beyond, perhaps, mentioning the high-camshaft mountings, the light-alloy connecting rods, the plain big-end bearings and the pressure-feed lubrication system.

The engine, which looks at first glance a single-cylinder, is so compact that it is housed without alteration of chain-line in the normal Triumph "Tiger 90" frame. Nor is there any need to add that it was with considerable anticipation that one of these machines was taken over for road test! It may be said right away that the machine submitted for test amply fulfilled the high claims made by its makers; its all-round performance was surprising.

No decompressor is fitted to the "Speed Twin" Triumph and none was found necessary, for the engine would start immediately under all conditions. When the engine was cold it was necessary to flood the carburettor and a fairly hearty kick was required. At all other times a gentle dig on the kick-starter would set the engine ticking over. With the ignition retarded the slow running was excellent and could be relied upon in traffic. At one period during the test the slow running disappeared, but this was quickly traced to a loose adjuster in the throttle cable.

Whether the engine was idling or on larger throttle openings, mechanical noise was very slight. At very low speeds a certain amount of mechanical noise could be heard, but this was no greater than that of a good 500 c.c. single at similar speeds. Once the machine was on the move all traces of mechanical sound disappeared and at high speeds the engine could not be heard even when the rider turned his head out of the air stream.

At no time was the exhaust noise objectionable; at low road speeds the exhaust was almost inaudible, while at speeds of 60 m.p.h. and over it developed into a pleasant low zoom.

So much then for general features of the machine. It is in the engine's performance that the real delight of the "Speed Twin" lies. So versatile did the engine

Gear.	Maximum Speeds.	Acceleration.	
		15-30 m.p.h.	20-50 m.p.h.
First (12.7)	46 m.p.h.	2⅔ secs.	—
Second (8.65)	62 m.p.h.	3⅜ secs.	6 secs.
Third (6.0)	80 m.p.h.	5 secs.	8⅜ secs.
Top (5.0)	93.75 m.p.h.	7 secs.	11¼ secs.

PERFORMANCE DATA.

Speed attained over ¼ mile through gears from standing start : 74 m.p.h.
Braking from 30 m.p.h. in top gear : 30 feet.
Fuel consumption at a maintained 40 m.p.h. : 82.2 m.p.g.
Minimum non-snatch speed in top gear : 12 m.p.h.

Models

The push-rod tubes are carried in the vees formed by the cylinders. Access to the tappets is gained by removing the screwed caps on the rocker boxes. The pipes leading from the rocker gear to the push-rod tubes are oil drains

prove that the machine was equally at home in the thickest traffic or on the fastest main road. In traffic it would trickle along perfectly happily at 20 m.p.h. in top gear, and would accelerate rapidly and smoothly from this speed. If need be, the engine, with the ignition retarded, could be throttled down to 12 m.p.h. in top gear without any transmission snatch. If the gears were used, acceleration well above average was available. To accelerate from 15 to 30 m.p.h. in bottom gear, for example, took only 2⅖ seconds. In second gear, the one normally used for hurried acceleration, less than four seconds was required. Even in top gear the time taken was only seven seconds.

Similarly on the open road, the acceleration was excellent, as a glance at the figures in the table shows.

On the Open Road

Much of the joy in driving the model comes, however, from the delightful way the machine will zoom from 30 m.p.h. to 60, 70 or 80 m.p.h. at the will of the rider without his having to touch any control other than the twist-grip. Some idea of the model's performance when the gears are used can be obtained from the fact that 74 m.p.h. was reached in a quarter of a mile from a standing start.

On the open road the machine was utterly delightful. Ample power for all conditions was always available at a turn of the twist-grip, and the lack of noise when the machine was cruising in the seventies was almost uncanny. Main road hills were taken in the model's stride with just a little more throttle opening, and even on very steep hills or on hills with sharp bends which necessitated a change down, the acceleration available

would rapidly bring the machine back to a high cruising speed. Thus it was found that large mileages were tucked into the hour without the rider consciously hurrying, and long runs were accomplished with less mental effort than usual.

Even when the performance figures already quoted are borne in mind, the sheer maximum speed of the machine is surprising. The timed tests were carried out on a day when there was a fair breeze blowing. With the rider clad in a single-piece "International" suit and lying well down along the tank (sitting on the mudguard, there being no pillion seat) the mean speed of four runs, two with and two against the wind, was 93.75 m.p.h.

The best timed run with the wind behind gave a speed over the quarter-mile of 107 m.p.h.—truly an

---

SPECIFICATION

TYPE : "Speed Twin" model.

ENGINE : 63 × 80 mm. (497 c.c.) vertical twin-cylinder o.h.v. Triumph with totally enclosed valve gear and dry-sump lubrication.

CARBURETTOR : Amal with special Triumph twist-grip control.

GEAR BOX : Triumph four-speed with enclosed foot change.

TRANSMISSION : Chain with primary oil bath and double rear chain guard.

IGNITION : Lucas Magdyno.

LIGHTING : Lucas 6-volt with voltage control and tank-top switch panel.

FUEL CAPACITY : 3¼ gals.

TYRES : Dunlop, 3.00—20 ribbed front ; 3.50—19 "Universal" rear.

GROUND CLEARANCE : 5in.

WEIGHT : 365 lb. fully equipped.

PRICE : £77 15s., with full electrical equipment and 120 m.p.h. illuminated speedometer.

MAKERS : Triumph Engineering Co., Coventry.

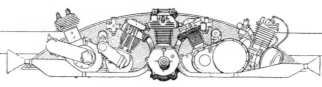

amazing figure for a fully equipped five-hundred. Moreover, so steady was the model at this speed that the rider found it difficult to realise that the machine was travelling so quickly. Naturally, the steering damper was tightened down for the tests of maximum speed, but at no other time was it used or found necessary.

The steering and handling of the machine on the road are excellent. The only criticism was that the rear wheel had a tendency to hop on uneven surfaces. Cornering and general manœuvrability proved to be of a very high order, and the model, with its low centre of gravity, felt more like a two-fifty than a five-hundred from the point of view of ease of handling.

It is extremely fortunate that the Triumph *is* so well-mannered, for owing to the smoothness and silence of the engine there was a distinct tendency for the rider to take corners at higher speeds than usual, but even on corners rounded at really high speeds the Triumph was perfectly steady and safe.

A high degree of balance has been achieved with the Triumph, and apart from a slight period around 60 m.p.h. in top gear the engine is perfectly smooth and sweet. It may even be said that the period is only noticeable because of the exceptional smoothness of the engine at all other speeds, and at no time was the vibration sufficient to cause any discomfort.

Well Chosen Ratios

The Triumph four-speed gear box was delightfully quiet on all gears. The clutch was free from drag and the gear change was light and positive.

The gear ratios are well chosen and the maximum speeds reached by the machine in the indirect gears were: Third (6 to 1), 80 m.p.h.; second (8.65 to 1), 62 m.p.h.; and bottom (12.7 to 1), 46 m.p.h. With regard to the figures for bottom and second gear, it should be mentioned that the engine at these speeds was being grossly over-revved.

For normal speeds and for persons of normal height

the riding position is good. The controls are well placed and the brake and gear lever pedals are in convenient positions. For a tall rider, however, the saddle is somewhat too near the handlebars. With the saddle moved back a little way it is probable that the tendency towards rear-wheel hop at high speeds would be overcome; at the same time the riding position would be improved. These remarks apply only to fast road work. At normal speeds the riding position is comfortable and the supple saddle and wide range of movement of the front forks successfully smooth out road shocks.

The new Triumph twist-grip with internal ratchet is pleasant in use, and all feeling of the ratchet is lost when the machine is on the road, yet the grip remains positive in action. On the model tested there was a tendency for the throttle to close if the hand was removed from the grip at high speeds.

Clean and Smart

As is to be expected with a machine of such a high general standard as the Triumph, the brakes proved to be first class. Both were extremely powerful and smooth, and applied together they would bring the model to rest from 30 m.p.h. in a fraction less than 30ft.

In economy the Triumph also scored, for at a maintained speed of 40 m.p.h. the petrol consumption was 82 m.p.g. A small trouble that occurred in the course of the test was the fracture of the angle bracket used for the attachment of the front end of the fuel tank.

Finally, mention must be made of the machine's appearance. The standard finish is amaranth red. It is a plum colour and looks extremely smart in conjunction with the chromium plating on other parts of the machine. At the conclusion of the test, which included hundreds of miles of really hard driving, the Triumph was as clean and smart as at the beginning, and apart from a very slight seep of oil from the rear end of the primary chain case, not a spot of oil had leaked from any of the joints of the power unit.

Glamour of the East

A Touring Episode Which Might Also be Entitled " What's in a Name? "

IN Oxfordshire, and not very far from Oxford itself, are two villages with the rather strange names of Britwell Salome and Berrick Salome. Years ago I noticed these curious names on a map and I promised myself that some day my B.S.A. would take me to these two out-of-the-way places.

The name Salome called up romantic visions of the glamorous East, of the beautiful dancer Salome, who in Biblical days danced for a man's head on a charger, and I used to wonder if these two villages embodied

in any way the exotic atmosphere of the Orient. . . .

And now I've been to see the Salome villages, and I can tell you that they don't. Somehow I'm sorry I went because I've lost an illusion. They are two ordinary villages similar to many others on this edge of the Chiltern Hills.

As for the name Salome, I've learnt that the name is believed to be derived from the old English " sulh," meaning a furrow. The place-name pundits are such unromantic fellows!   H. L. B.

High = Performance
Overhead=Valve Five=
Hundred with Many
Outstanding Features

This sectional drawing of
the new 497 c.c. twin reveals
the detail construction and,
incidentally, shows the
sturdy nature of the various
components. The cylinders
are cast in one block and
the push rod tubes are
carried in the vees formed
by the two cylinders. Note
the ingenious built - up
crankshaft, with its central
flywheel, and the method of
valve gear enclosure

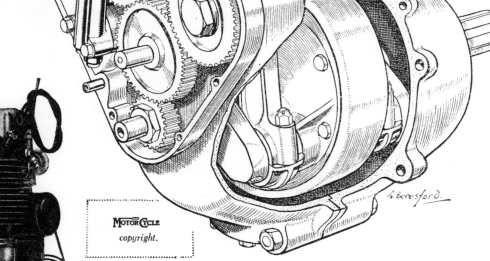

MotorCycle
copyright.

A feature of the new Triumph vertical
twin is the unusually rigid crankcase. The
overall width of the crank unit is actually
slightly less than that of the Tiger " 90 "
single-cylinder model. Access to the valve-
clearance adjusters is obtained via the
caps screwed into the rocker box

VERTICAL TWIN

TRIUMPH

Road Tests of 1939 Models

THE 500 c.c. o.h.

(Below) To all intents and purposes the twin Triumph looks like a neat single, the high speed vertical engine being housed comfortably in the frame. (Right, in circle) The drive side of the unit, showing the oil bath primary chain case of cast aluminium with accessible filler-cap.

Horsepower of two ages! The oldest form of mobile motive power used by man looks with a kindly eye on its most modern descendant.

LAST year's Speed Twin Triumph was undoubtedly an exceptional machine, but the 1939 Tiger "100," which is a development of it, can be called without exaggeration a "super" job. In top gear 10 m.p.h. to 98 m.p.h. were the figures obtained last week from a production machine in the hands of one of *Motor Cycling's* testers, a combination of docility and all-out performance which demonstrates in no uncertain manner that speed can be obtained from a well-designed twin without sacrificing that flexibility which is so necessary on a road-going motorcycle.

Steering

High performance is no use unless it is easily controlled, so a new frame and altered front forks were designed by Mr. E. Turner, which have made the Tiger "100" into a mount with steering and handling beyond reproach under any conditions. Riding really fast on the open road or pottering about in thick traffic inspired the greatest confidence right from the word "go." Truly it is a difficult matter to offer any criticisms on this latest product of the Triumph Engineering Co., Ltd., which seems to combine all those qualities which motorcyclists have hoped for but seldom actually experienced.

The design of the power unit is by now so well known that there is little need to mention any details; suffice

A Flexible Multi Capable of Nearly 100 m.p.h.

to say that the cylinders are placed side by side transversely and are so neatly laid out that it needs more than a casual glance to see whether it be a two-port single or a twin.

As the performance figures of the Tiger "100" are probably the first facts our readers want to know, we will start by stating the results which were obtained against the stop-watch. The best timed speed over the flying quarter-mile was 97.83 m.p.h., and the mean of two runs in each direction turned out very nearly as good—95.74 m.p.h.—most excellent results, which are all the more creditable when it is remembered that the machine was fully equipped with efficient silencers, lights, dynamo, tools, and all the other items necessary for touring.

The acceleration was little short of breathtaking, so much power being available that great care had to be exercised with the clutch when getting off the mark. The figure obtained for the standing quarter-mile was 15¾ secs., which is an average of 56.96 m.p.h., and at the end of the distance the speed reached was over

TWIN TIGER "100"
TRIUMPH

Cornering on the Tiger " 100" was always safe and certain.

hours. No particular effort was made to go very quickly, but when a machine settles down to high-speed cruising it is simple to cover 50 miles in an hour. On twisty secondary roads the Tiger was equally delightful, and if proper use was made of the gearbox high speeds could be maintained, although it was this type of going which enabled one to appreciate the smooth power which was available in top gear from 30 m.p.h. onwards. Riding quite normally, the best speeds to change up were 40 m.p.h. and 60 m.p.h. respectively from second to third and third to top. This gear-changing was child's play, the travel of the lever being short and the selection absolutely positive.

On Tricky Roads

Closely allied to such easy high-speed travel was the excellent steering and handling of the machine. It is no exaggeration to say that it was a genuine pleasure to motor really fast round corners. No need to worry on a strange road what would happen when the road surface changed suddenly from good to bad, the Tiger " 100" was certain to do the right thing. Hump-backed bridges could be "jumped" with impunity, the model being warranted to land straight and stay straight. Round corners of all types, bumpy, smooth, fast or slow, the machine could be laid right over almost until the footrests touched. Most convincing of all, it was a genuine pleasure to ride the Triumph round Brooklands at 90 m.p.h., as it steered to a hair and gave a most comfortable ride.

Special mention must be made of the fine pair of brakes. They were both so effective that either wheel could be locked on dry concrete with a medium pressure, but the action was so progressive that only clumsiness could be blamed for such a thing occurring. The figure of 28 ft. from 30 m.p.h. being rated at over 100 per cent. efficient leaves little to be desired.

Another point concerning comfort was the new shape of handlebar. Nice and narrow, with grips placed just right for real comfort and easy handling, the bar and its

80 m.p.h. In the gears some more astonishing readings were recorded, 90 m.p.h. and 66 m.p.h. being attained in third and second respectively, at which speeds the engine was turning round at over 7,000 r.p.m.

Throughout the whole range the balance was remarkably good, although between 70 m.p.h. and 75 m.p.h. in third there was a certain amount of vibration, a period which was overcome when the latter speed was exceeded. Somewhat naturally, the same symptoms were evident at corresponding revolution per minute in second gear. In top gear the engine seemed to smooth itself out and the unit was delightfully silky at all normal touring speeds. One fact which we have omitted to mention is that the Tiger " 100" lapped Brooklands at a shade over 92 m.p.h.—a remarkable performance.

So much for the maximum figures; equally impressive were the lowest non-snatch speeds, which were 10 m.p.h., 8 m.p.h. and 6 m.p.h. respectively in top, third and second gears. With the ignition retarded the machine would travel slowly along a level road and smoothly accelerate away by judicious use of the throttle.

On the road something over 300 miles were covered, embracing fast stretches where cruising speeds of 80 m.p.h. were possible, slow country lanes and twisty secondary roads. Under all these varying conditions the most striking thing was the effortless manner in which the miles were covered. The run to Brooklands from Coventry, 104 miles, was completed in well under two

Brief Specification of the 500 c.c. o.h.v. Triumph Tiger "100"

Engine: Vertical twin o.h.v. double high camshaft, 63 mm. bore by 80 mm. stroke = 498 c.c. Crankshaft mounted on ball bearings with central flywheel. Pressure lubrication to plain bearing big-ends, RR 56 connecting rods, with split big-ends, having steel caps white metal lined. Large-bore Amal carburetter.

Frame: Full cradle with taper front down tube. Taper tube girder forks with central compression spring and quickly adjustable damper on the lower bridge.

Transmission: Four-speed foot-operated Triumph gearbox. Ratios: 5.0, 6.0, 8.65 and 12.70 to 1. Primary chain in aluminium oilbath. Rear chain protected by guard and lubricated from the oilbath.

Wheels: Triumph. Tyre sections: 26 by 3.00 ribbed front, 26 by 3.50 Speed Universal rear. 7-in. diameter brakes front and rear.

Tanks: Welded-steel oil and fuel. Oil, 1 gallon. Fuel, 4 gallons, with tank panel carrying oil gauge, ammeter and lighting switch

Dimensions: Saddle height (standard), 27¾ ins. Wheelbase, 54 ins. Overall length, 84 ins. Overall width, 28½ ins. Ground clearance, 5 ins.

Weight: Fully equipped, 1 gallon of oil, but no fuel, 371 lb.

Price: £80.

Extra: £2 15s., Smith's chronometric trip speedometer.

Makers: The Triumph Engineering Co., Ltd., Coventry.

Tax: £2 5s. per annum.

TIGER "100" ROAD TEST (Contd.)

controls are adjustable, but the standard position proved the best for our tester.

Starting the engine, either hot or cold, was a job that required little or no skill. The air lever could be left in the open position and ignored on all occasions. When cold, the carburetter needed a little flooding, the ignition setting at about two-thirds advance and a first-kick start was certain with the throttle slightly open. When hot the procedure was the same except that no flooding was necessary.

Fuel consumption, motoring fast on long runs, came out at just under 60 m.p.g., whilst accurate tests on the open road and in dense traffic produced figures of 63 m.p.g. and 57 m.p.g. respectively; very good results when the performance of the machine is taken into account. Oil consumption was negligible, there being no appreciable difference between the level before and after 300 miles, therefore draining and refilling the tank at the recommended periods would represent the only cost in oil. The complete absence of any oil leakage, either from the engine or gearbox, indicates that long periods can be anticipated between any major cleaning operations.

The noise problem has received careful attention; mechanically, both the engine and gearbox scored full marks, as riding at any speed over 35 m.p.h. they were practically inaudible. The exhaust was extremely quiet on all normal throttle openings, but a healthy roar came forth when the taps were opened wide. This is not surprising when the power output is taken into account.

Maintenance of any sort was not necessary whilst the machine was in our hands, but all the usual points were checked over and the normal tool kit appeared quite adequate. The primary chain is adjusted by removing the off-side footrest and pushing the spindle out of the way. The clamping nut can then be loosened and the adjuster moved as required.

A reasonable distance was covered by night and the lights gave excellent results. The head lamp beam was powerful and well distributed over the whole width of a main road, also the voltage control regulated the charging rate in the approved manner. Illumination was automatically provided for the speedometer as soon as the lights were switched on, and a dash light enabled the ammeter and oil gauge to be read. It would be an improvement if this last-mentioned light were provided with a switch, as it was sufficiently bright to catch one's eye when riding and it wasted current when the machine was parked with the lights on.

The speedometer is ingenious, having three inner circles which are calibrated in r.p.m. corresponding to the road speeds in top, third and second gears.

Silver in colour, with a beautifully polished aluminium chain case and all the necessary parts chromium plated, the Tiger "100" would attract one's attention on account of its looks, let alone the outstanding performance already described. The price fully equipped is £80, the only extra being the 120 m.p.h. Smith's speedometer, which costs £2 15s.

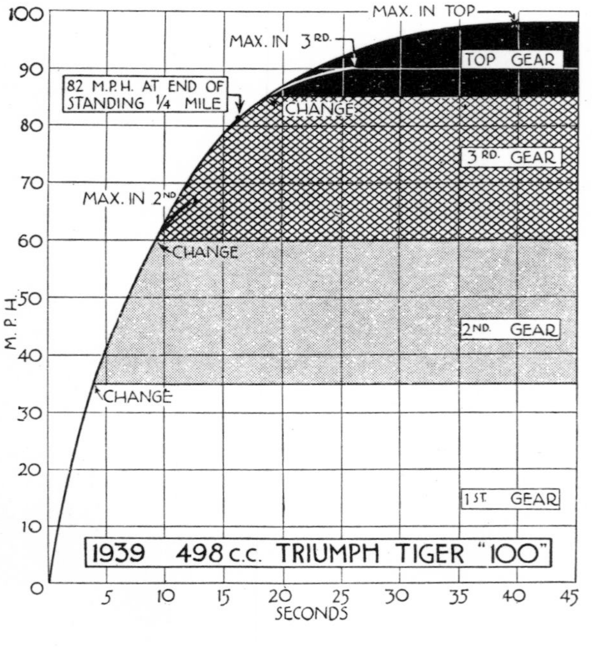
MAX. IN TOP
MAX. IN 3RD.
TOP GEAR
82 M.P.H. AT END OF STANDING ¼ MILE
CHANGE
3RD. GEAR
MAX. IN 2ND.
CHANGE
2ND. GEAR
CHANGE
1ST GEAR
M.P.H.
100
90
80
70
60
50
40
30
20
10
0
5
10
15
20
25
30
35
40
45
SECONDS
1939 498 c.c. TRIUMPH TIGER "100"

MOTOR CYCLING

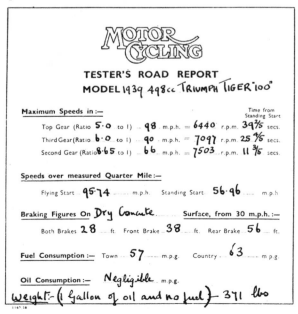

TESTER'S ROAD REPORT

MODEL 1939 498cc TRIUMPH TIGER "100"

Maximum Speeds in :— Time from Standing Start

Top Gear (Ratio 5·0 to 1) 98 m.p.h. = 6440 r.p.m. 39⅘ secs.

Third Gear (Ratio 6·0 to 1) 90 m.p.h. = 7097 r.p.m. 25⅘ secs.

Second Gear (Ratio 8·65 to 1) 66 m.p.h. = 7503 r.p.m. 11⅗ secs.

Speeds over measured Quarter Mile :—

Flying Start 95·74 m.p.h. Standing Start 56·96 m.p.h.

Braking Figures On Dry Concrete **Surface, from 30 m.p.h. :—**

Both Brakes 28 ft. Front Brake 38 ft. Rear Brake 56 ft.

Fuel Consumption :— Town 57 m.p.g. Country 63 m.p.g.

Oil Consumption :— Negligible m.p.g.

Weight:- (1 Gallon of oil and no fuel) - 371 lbs

DESIGNED FOR ARMY WORK

On one of the now very high rock steps. The light weight of the special Triumph makes it remarkably easy to handle on rough going

DESIGNED by Mr. Edward Turner as, in his opinion, the motor cycle for the Army. Of course, the idea of a 350 c.c. vertical-twin Triumph is not new. Such a machine was a natural corollary to the Speed Twin, and its hyper-sports sister, the Tiger 100, and the week war broke out a number of readers were puzzled by the fact that their copies of *The Motor Cycle* bore on the cover the words "New 350 c.c. British Twin," yet not a line on the subject appeared in our columns. What had occurred was that the exclusive description of the new Triumph vertical-twin, which had already been passed for press, had to be lifted out because of the war.

This was at the last moment, and it was impossible to reprint all the covers in the time available, so a few—a very few—announced a twin that was never described!

Left to the Manufacurers

The complete article is still in page form. Perhaps one day it will be released. But the machine concerned is markedly different from the model Mr. Turner has designed as his ideal Army motor cycle. The authorities laid down weight limits, but left it to the chosen manufacturers as to what was produced. Wisely, they wanted the industry's ideas. Some years earlier their predecessors had tried their hands at laying out a machine.

The Triumph managing director had long been interested in power/weight ratios. He is also essentially a production engineer. Briefly, what he had in mind in laying out a machine for W.D. work was:—

(1) That it should be fundamentally light so that it could be manhandled over obstacles or dragged out of shell holes; (2) start easily; (3) be eminently flexible and tractable, but have a performance that would enable it to cover the

ground really quickly when necessary; (4) give 10,000 miles of comprehensive service under the worst conditions before overhaul was needed and without the need for constant maintenance; (5) do all this, yet the machine be easier and cheaper to produce than anything comparable.

The resultant machine was subjected to the usual 10,000 miles test at the Mechanization Experimental Establishment with (to quote the official Ministry of Supply statement) "very satisfactory results." I, during a visit to the Establishment, tried the machine. It proved enthralling —lively, mettlesome; in fact, just the motor cycle to appeal to the lads of the village. Of performance below about 3,000 r.p.m. the engine had next to none. Knowing a little of Army work and requirements, I could not see this motor cycle proving suitable. I said so, and, in our issue of August 1st, 1940, took it upon myself to write a leader, "The New Army Lightweights: Not all have the characteristics best suited to Army work: Wisdom dictates that the model (or models) standardised should not be rushed into large-scale production but a batch made under actual production conditions and issued to the Service."

I had the 350 c.c. Triumph Twin particularly in mind. Frankly, I did not consider that the machine could be made really suitable. While a twin, in my experience, requires considerably less maintenance than the equivalent single, and has useful advantages for Army work in this connection, I have not found that it obtains the same wheel-grip on loose surfaces and in mud as a single; with a four there is apt to be more spin still, and an even greater difficulty in getting away on a slippery hill. And this twin had revs and plenty of power at revs, but no real slogging ability.

Now that I have tried the machine which has been de-

A 400=mile Test of a 350 c.c. Unit=construction Vertical=twin Triumph— a Lightweight Solo as Controllable as an Autocycle and as Lively as a "Speed Twin"

By ARTHUR BOURNE, Editor of *The Motor Cycle*

veloped from the subimago I am amazed. What follow are superlatives. I make no apology. A member of the staff to whom I said, "Take it round the houses; it's going back to-morrow," arrived back in my office, brought his cup of tea in with him, sat down, and said, "It's a revelation!"

However, let us start at the beginning of my 400-mile test—begin with a quick look over the machine. The weight-saving has been achieved by design. I cannot say how all the parts would stand up to week-after-week service in the Army's hands. It seems to me, however, that the designer has been at pains to leave an ample margin of strength, and there is nothing which, in the unlikely event of it giving trouble under unexpected stresses, could not be strengthened or altered to suit. Indeed, there are parts which appear to me unnecessarily robust for a machine with two 175 c.c. cylinders. The weight, incidentally, is 263 lb. Before the edict that less use must be made of light alloys it was some 230 lb., with all tools, lighting, tanks full and so on—yes, 230 lb.!

Primarily, the reason for the stipulation of light weight was, as you know, ease of handling and manhandling. The Army motor cyclist's job is to get there irrespective of the conditions. The low weight has other advantages, as will be seen.

The chief features of the design are the twin-cylinder

The power unit is exceptionally neat and compact. Note the rocker box integral with the cylinder heads, the air control on the carburettor and the light-alloy footrest. The pedal is, of course, the foot-change, while to the rear of the gear box is the tool box. The generator for the direct lighting protrudes slightly from the timing chest

o.h.v. engine, with its unit-construction three-speed gear box, a duplex flat-link primary chain with a set-screw adjusted skate tensioner, a patented form of tank construction that embodies a U-shaped longitudinal member and acts as the top tube of the frame (and, incidentally, gives a really large tank capacity), direct lighting from a small A.C. generator in the timing cover, an air filter merged neatly and accessibly in the oil tank (which causes slight preheating of the air), and a B.T-H. magneto that

Muddy, but running as perfectly as ever —a glimpse of the 350 c.c. vertical-twin Triumph which Mr. Turner has designed as his idea of *the* Army machine. Unit construction, with a flat-backed duplex chain is employed. The two cylinders exhaust into a single, very efficient silencer

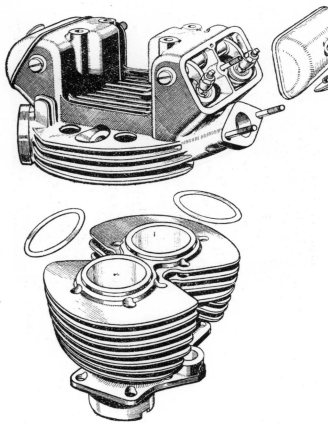

(Left) The rocker boxes are cast with the cylinder heads, thereby avoiding oil leaks and minimising uneven expansion. Single fixing studs retain the covers. The cylinders are cast together

No exhaust valve lifter is fitted, but the individual cylinder capacity is only 175 c.c., so there is not the slightest difficulty in kicking over the engine even when the temperature is below freezing. The air control consists of a spring-loaded plunger on the air slide, which is held down for starting from cold by an internal bayonet catch. Apparently I did not get the throttle setting cum degree of flooding quite weighed up, for in the cold weather that was usual during the test, generally half a dozen digs at the starter pedal were necessary before the engine continued to fire.

My first run included traffic work and much wet wood paving. The machine is as controllable as an autocycle.

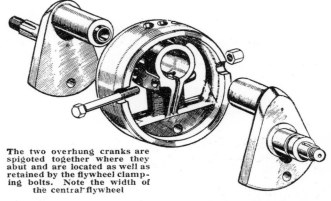

The two overhung cranks are spigoted together where they abut and are located as well as retained by the flywheel clamping bolts. Note the width of the central flywheel

incorporates an automatic advance-and-retard. Other points are rocker boxes cast integrally with the cylinder heads, tension springs with rocking levers as the fork dampers, a large tool-box sensibly mounted low down (behind the gear box), 3.25-19 tyres and rear fork-ends welded on the simple rear-frame members, which, as will be seen from the photographs, are swept forward to the front of the engine-gear unit.

Apart from the lightness that has been achieved as a consequence of the engine being a 350 c.c. twin—the very light gear box and engine plates and the light hubs, etc.—a considerable saving has been effected by making the whole machine small. Throughout the design great care has been taken to save cost in the form of material and labour—to ensure, in times like these, true ease of production.

I know of no fully fledged motor cycle on which it would be as easy to teach anyone to ride. The machine's flexibility is almost uncanny. With the engine warm I got off the machine when it was in top gear (5.89 to 1) and trotted—*not* ran—beside it with the engine still firing evenly. For all normal purposes it is a top-gear machine. The one control, except for traffic lights and the like, is the throttle. Right-angle corners are taken on the throttle alone. The engine has been transformed: there is smooth, effortless power right from almost countable r.p.m. up to the machine's maximum. The throttle opens up absolutely cleanly. There is no "woosh" of power unless you specifically demand it by snapping the throttle open, but just an admirable gradual opening up with every one of the unnoticeable clicks in the spring-plunger-and-pinion twist-grip, causing additional power.

This surprising and delightful docility is far from being at the expense of acceleration. The final edition of the 350 Twin I have recently tested is the nippiest machine of its size I have ever tried. Quite early on I had found that in getting off the mark it would hold practically anything on wheels. The driver of a big American coupé tried his best on one occasion; on another it was the driver of a reputedly super-sports British car. Even in the case of the big American, which is of a type that shows some of the best acceleration figures in *The Autocar* Road Tests, the twin was ahead until approximately 60 m.p.h. was reached. Later, as a matter of interest, I roughly checked the top-gear acceleration from 20 to 50 m.p.h. The mean time was approximately 12.6 seconds, which beats all but one of the sixteen 1939 model motor cycles we tested in our Road Test series—a series that included six five-hundreds and one six-hundred. This was with my big bulk in the saddle.

That low weight means another thing: the machine

A single nut holds the twisted-wire-type air cleaner in place. The carburettor intake is linked to the duct in the oil tank by means of a rubber moulding

whisks round corners; and a third point, that the machine is utterly controllable. The sole skid I had, other than on rough-stuff, was when taking up the very obvious challenge from the British car just mentioned. On the wet surface, with the flat-out acceleration, the machine started to broadside. It came to heel without the slightest difficulty. Not only does this lightweight make the rider feel he is the master, but he *is*.

The gear change is now good, but in an upward direction slow unless one is to clash the gears slightly. The correct thing when changing up is very leisurely to raise the right toes; then the gears engage without a sound. The three speeds provided are all that are needed. Except for the superb acceleration available in second (9.67 to 1) being worth while at times (and adding to the rider's *joie de vivre!*), a mere two-speed gear would probably be ample, so flexible, yet lively, is the engine.

A point about the Triumph, with its silencer based, I gather, on the recent research by the National Physical Laboratory, is its high degree of exhaust silence, which has always seemed to me a most desirable feature of any machine for military purposes. The engine is also commendably quiet mechanically.

Having satisfied myself that the twin had no vices under traffic conditions—far from it—the next thing was an open road trip and plenty of rough-stuff. I thought in terms of Somerset and North Devon The idea of the twin climbing Porlock like the proverbial scalded cat was appealing. The day the thought occurred was spring-like. The

A small throttle opening, back wheel spinning on an "impossible" surface—the machine is walked upwards without any real heaving

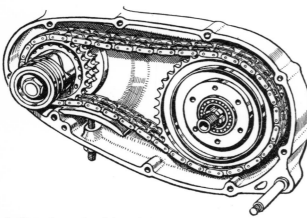

A slipper is employed for adjustment of the flat-backed duplex primary chain. This arrangement has proved very satisfactory in practice

following morning, just after black-out was over, I wheeled out the machine. Porlock it should be. The temperature was below freezing point, but no doubt as soon as the sun rose the conditions would be more comfortable.

At the end of the first 20 miles the machine was coated with patches of ice, so was my riding coat, while my moustache was frozen solid. Visibility at times was no more than 20 yards. I stopped, fumbled for my pipe, and communed with myself. So far I had averaged approximately 24 m.p.h. What chance of making Devon, doing all I intended down there, and getting home by nightfall? The answer was, if the conditions prevailed, none!

Instead I decided upon a 150-mile ramble that would include fast work (if the weather improved) and just about every type of rough-stuff.

For the next dozen miles the going should have been very fast, but there was still the vile mist. I dived down a side turning to make for an area of hills and mud. A column of Army vehicles was using the same route. Very

appropriate, for it would be much the same sort of riding as that which faces the R.A.S.C. motor cyclists—overhauling a convoy, nipping in and out. The zipping acceleration, ease of handling and excellent braking were just the thing: speedy overtaking with utter safety.

Later I got right off the beaten track and into rutted lanes. The reason why the ruts in one track were so deep was timber-hauling. Blocking the way from bank to bank was a truck. A flick of the throttle and the Triumph had climbed the foot-high bank on the left. It was round and on the track again without a moment lost. Had I not attempted some bank-climbing with one of the earlier lightweight twins I should not have dreamed of charging the bank. With the Triumph it was so supremely easy that even I never thought of waving a foot.

Next was a juicy mud section. I knew that no motor cycle was likely to get up here unaided, for not very long ago one of the greatest experts in the land could not manage it, and on the present occasion there had been the overnight frost. Whether any machine of equivalent size—and fitted with the same not very rugged type of tyre tread—would have got more wheelgrip I do not know, but by my endeavouring to keep the throttle down to somewhere near the amount of grip available the Triumph,

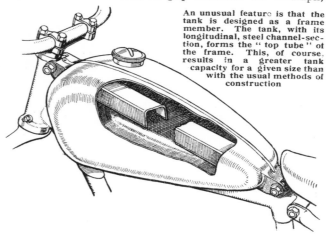

An unusual feature is that the tank is designed as a frame member. The tank, with its longitudinal, steel channel-section, forms the "top tube" of the frame. This, of course, results in a greater tank capacity for a given size than with the usual methods of construction

(Left) Steel-backed lead-bronze bushes are employed for the little-end bearings and white metal for the big-ends

(Right) Rutted mud, slippery tracks—all come the same to the Triumph with its low weight and exceptional ease of handling

thanks to that now remarkable low-speed pulling, got very much farther than I expected. Then I was able to do something which, I believe, would have been quite beyond me with a heavy machine, namely, walk the machine upwards. Incidentally, thanks to the light weight, I had been able to check all the previous plunges with genteel tip-toe-like dabs.

The rock hill which was the next inclusion was worse than I have known it. It is a hill to which I introduced the Mechanization Establishment some 2½ years ago, and methinks they have recently been using it for vehicles very different from motor cycles. The rock outcrops were more prominent than ever, and the mud all churned up. I decided to attempt an Army-type climb—I thought it would be safer!—so at the first provocation out went my two feet. At one point there was a crash of crankcase undershield on rock; the 5in. ground clearance was not equal to that particular outcrop. The model gently worked its way upwards without any effort on my part, just the capabilities required and, so far as I am concerned, mutt into nigh-to-expert.

What would happen on the descent, as there was no exhaust lifter control? I have found this can be a definite snag when rough-stuffing with Fours. In this case the engine, with its slow, even tick over, and bottom gear (15.97 to 1) engaged, seemed to provide a little smooth braking Anyhow, the lack of an exhaust-valve lifter did not worry me here or elsewhere.

Already there had been four minor watersplashes. Now there was another deeper one, followed by a slithery climb. Everything is nicely high on the Triumph and the plugs, in any case, have K.L.G. waterproof covers, so I can imagine no trouble if a splash is taken sensibly. On the hill I had to do some foot-slogging owing to lack of wheel-grip. It was light because of the excellent slow pulling of the engine and the fact that the machine is light.

Tacks of various types followed, some sandy and others deeply rutted mud. The machine handled as only one of low weight can. I tried the steering lock, which I had already noted as being exceptionally good. The Triumph will turn round in a single swing on a lane that will barely take an Army lorry.

It seemed that nearly enough had been done on hills to determine whether there was justification for the term "go anywhere." However, not very far away was a 1 in 4½ climb with a good surface. A little restarting might be worth trying. In bottom gear the machine simply shot off the mark on the steepest pitch. Wet chalk tracks

came a little later, all bringing out the machine's exceptional ease of control.

Now for main road work. An earlier machine had been terrier-with-a-rat at the front end, and I had told Mr. Turner bluntly that I did not like the front fork action. This final edition steers excellently.

Driving around 60 m.p.h. did not worry the machine one atom. There was just a happy drone. Open up at this speed—there is an unexpected amount of throttle left —and there is still really excellent pick-up. Even with my large multi-coated body upright the machine topped seventy on the level with ease—not once but many times. Officially, I believe, the maximum is around 75 m.p.h. Consumption? I checked off with a measured gallon. On mixed riding—traffic work and some fairly fast open-road riding—the distance covered was some 75 miles.

Main road hills are levelled in the manner of a much larger-engined machine. A twitch of the throttle and up goes the speed from 50 to 55 or 55 to 60 even on quite useful upgrades. The revs seem unlimited. Once in a rather disgraceful moment I let the speed mount to well over 50 m.p.h. in second gear, which, as this is 9.67 to 1, meant some 6,500 r.p.m. Throughout the speed range the balance is excellent.

The riding position is a good compromise. The bolted-on light-alloy footrests are non-adjustable and, if you ride on your toes, the kick-starter pedal fouls your right leg. This would apparently be obviated if the pedal was arranged to come into action later in its stroke, which would, in any case, be an advantage as regards starting. After 150 miles that included much rough going I was a little stiff, largely, I think, because of the hardness of the particular saddle. The cut-out button on the contact-breaker end of the B.T.-H. magneto does not leave a lot of room for a large gloved hand, and I, with my on-the-toes riding, large feet and, perhaps, peculiar riding position, scorched my left wader on the near-by exhaust pipe.

Of other criticisms—even tuppeny-ha'penny ones such as these last—I have none. This machine has all the good traits of the W.D. Douglas of the last war, plus power, remarkable acceleration, speed and general nippiness. I cannot visualise a motor cycle that in light of present knowledge would be better for the purpose for which it was designed. That I also consider it is far and away the best Triumph yet produced, and a machine with an outstanding appeal to both sportsmen and potterers is in present circumstances rather beside the point. What would it cost in the present form? Mr. Turner tells me that the machine would be offered to the Government at a lower price than that of the 350 c.c. W.D. side-valve Triumph single!

Road Tests of 1946 Models

The 498 c
Speed Tw
TRI

(Left) Thanks to the new Triumph telescopic forks, the Speed Twin can be handled easily at speed on the rough.

The Post-war Edition of a World-Famous British "Multi" is Put Through Its Paces

THIS being the first post-war "Motor Cycling" road test, it is perhaps fitting that it should concern a Triumph, for this famous Coventry factory was amongst the first to be ready for production with peace-time machines. Not only that, but the 1946 Triumph programme is, in actual fact, a new-model range in the full sense of the phrase. Mr. Edward Turner planned his programme well in advance, and when the moment came to make the change-over from war output to that of civilian production he was ready, not only to leave military models to the military, but to come out straight away with a series of mounts that represent logical progress over the years.

Thus it was that when "Motor Cycling" mooted the question of a road-test machine he was able to offer us the choice of four models, none of which is in any way a radical departure, but all of which are genuine "new season" types.

We had the pick of the Tiger 100, the new 350 vertical twin (in sports and touring trim) and the famous Speed Twin. A difficult choice it was, but after due consideration we took over a 1946 edition of the 498 c.c. Speed Twin for these reasons: It has been the most popular model in the Triumph catalogue since its introduction in 1937 and we road tested it twice before the war (in 1937 and 1939). It would be a good thing, therefore, we thought, to complete the hat trick, even if it comes nearly seven years late.

The specification changes in the latest Triumph machines have already been dealt with ("Motor Cycling," March 1 1945): in brief, they may be recapitulated as they have a considerable bearing on the performance experienced. Most

(Below) Waiting for it . . .! With revs mounting and clutch ready to go in, the tester is about to put the Triumph at the standing quarter.

outstanding of all, of course, is the adoption of telescopic forks, which in themselves bring about a change in front brake operation, head lamp support and, obviously, general appearance. Another immediately noticeable improvement is the employment of a four-gallon tank in place of the three-gallon container of previous years. Closer inspection reveals that lighting current is now generated by a separate dynamo, gear-driven direct from the forward camshaft and supported through the engine-plates behind the

front down tube. A twin-cylinder B.T.H. magneto in the normal position supplies the sparks. Another external change is in the shifting of the speedometer drive from front to rear wheel. Also, the keen-eyed comparator will notice that the head lamp is of smaller and neater dimensions and has its body finished in amaranth red to match the rest of the machine.

The engine itself has had its always tidy appearance improved by the removal of the external oil drain pipes which used to lead from the rocker

(Right) The lines of the machine are clean and attractive. With its polished chrome and aluminium, amaranth red cellulose and freedom from "hung - on etceteras," the Triumph twin is a mount for the connoisseur.

PH

Below is seen (left) the instrument panel on the tank (note also Motor Cycling's "remote control stop-watch mounting) and (bottom) an impression of the well-balanced layout of the Triumph when viewed "head-on."

boxes to the push-rod enclosing tubes. This oil return system is now completely internal, drillings in the head and barrel providing the necessary passageways.

There are also several changes in design which, though not apparent at a glance, nevertheless contribute considerably towards better performance and enhanced appearance. For example, it has been possible to reduce the handlebar controls to a minimum by dispensing with air and ignition levers, leaving only clutch and brake levers and dipper, horn and ignition switch buttons on the bars. A spring-loaded plunger now controls the air-slide in the carburetter directly (it is needed only for starting up from cold in extremely severe weather), while advance and retard of the magneto is taken care of by an automatic centrifugal device incorporated in the drive.

Finally, there is one more important factor which requires a word or two on its own. The compression ratio has been reduced from the previous $7\frac{1}{4}$ to $6\frac{1}{2}$ to 1. This has been done specifically to suit the Speed Twin engine to the grade of "Pool" petrol available at the present time. Triumphs looked at things this way. By providing a manually adjustable magneto and air-slide it would have been possible to say that the 1946 Twin, in the hands of a fully experienced rider, could achieve pre-war performance at the upper end of the speed scale on "Pool" petrol and on the old ratio. But primarily the Twin is intended for the man who first of all wants smooth running and *effortless* riding; he is more concerned with good all-round performance than the ultra-fast motoring which is, anyway, in the sphere of the Tiger 100.

No, Mr. Turner believes that the Speed Twin has got all the speed, and more, that the average rider needs and he is quite prepared to cast away a knot or two if in so doing he can achieve, on an inferior grade of fuel, a performance even smoother and a machine even nearer his ideal of efficient simplicity than he had in the earlier models.

And now let us leave discussion and get out on the road with this fascinating, amaranthine beauty. Dusk was approaching as we started up in the forecourt of Triumph's brand-new factory, so the first 30 or 40 miles as far as Malvern were taken restfully and smoothly with the rider contentedly revelling in the wonderful sensation of once more being on a real "civvy" motorcycle on a real English highway.

Travelling, then, at an easy pace over well-nigh-perfect roads it was not possible to assess the potentialities of the new-type springing, but it needed only a few miles to reach the conclusion that so far as open-road steering went here was something very well worth investigation. Accordingly next morning the Triumph was put to her first and perhaps most important test —how did she handle generally at a fastish clip over typical give-and-take main and secondary roads?

With Cheltenham as the next objective, a deliberately circuitous course was chosen with the idea of including not only the fast, straight stretches of the Bristol road, but also some winding loopways in flat, open Severn-side country where a model can be laid over to full and safe advantage.

It is doubtful if a motorcycling journalist has a harder professional task than to try to describe in bare words a man's feelings when he finds himself astride a machine which ideally suits him. How can mere writing express that sense of mastery, that sympathy with the machine, that exhilarating impression of *complete control* which a healthy engine, hair-fine steering and super-adequate braking can combine to inspire?

A Challenge Accepted

Small wonder, then, that the driver of a cheeky little sports car found his challenge accepted on a straight near Gloucester. It was rather like taking pennies from a blind man, but the mood was on and the Speed Twin has got something down in that sturdy double-hearted engine that just had to be used.

Having satisfied ourselves (and the sportsman in the car) that of fine-line cornering, V.2 getaway and "all-astern" stopping power we had plenty, we now tried a different tack and headed into the Cotswolds in search of that old Colmore Trial favourite, Mill Lane.

It would be useless to claim a clean climb (there were others present anyway!) but this can be said for the Speed Twin: its behaviour over the climbable parts of Mill Lane and on the byways in the vicinity was not only a delight to the rider but an eye-opener for

BRIEF SPECIFICATION OF THE 498 c.c. TRIUMPH SPEED TWIN

Engine: Vertical twin o.h.v.; double high camshaft, 63 mm. bore by 80 mm. stroke; compression ratio 6.5 to 1; dry sump lubrication; totally enclosed valves with duplex Aero springs; high-tensile aluminium alloy crankcase; H-section connecting rods in R.R. 56 Hiduminium alloy; crankshaft mounted on heavy-duty ball bearings, B.T.H. magneto with automatic control; Amal, carburetter, with Triumph patent quick-action twist-grip.

Transmission: Four speeds; foot-operated gearbox; ratios, 5.0, 6.0, 8.65 and 12.7 to 1; primary chain enclosed in streamlined polished aluminium oilbath; rear chain positively lubricated and provided with protection for both top and bottom runs.

Frame: Brazed-up, full cradle; special alloy steel; large diameter tapered front down-tube; spring-up rear stand; clip-up front stand.

Front Forks: Patent Triumph telescopic with large movement; hydraulically damped; automatically lubricated; integral head-lamp brackets.

Wheels: Triumph design; laced spokes; Dunlop tyres of 26-in. by 3.25-in. section front and 26-in. by 3.50-in. section rear, with security bolt; 7-in. diameter brakes; finger adjustment front and rear.

Tanks: All-welded steel petrol tank, capacity 4 gallons, with reserve tap; flush fitting, rubber-mounted instrument panel, carrying oil-gauge, ammeter, switch and dash-lamp; quick-opening filler; welded steel oil tank with accessible filters, drain-plug and separate vent; capacity, 1 gallon.

Dimensions: Saddle height, 27¾ ins.; wheelbase, 54 ins.; overall length, 84 ins.; overall width, 28½ ins.; ground clearance, 5 ins.

Weight: 365 lb.

Finish: Amaranth red cellulose and chrome; die-cast name plates, gilt finished, screwed to tank panels.

Price: £110 (plus £30 5s. purchase tax), fully equipped with separate Lucas dynamo lighting (6-v) with voltage control, 7-in. diameter head lamp and horn; special Triumph recessed kneegrips, adjustable de luxe saddle, downswept exhaust pipes; Triumph "safety" front number plate.

Extra: Smith 100 m.p.h. trip rear-driven speedometer, £3 10s. (plus 19s. 3d. purchase tax).

Makers: Triumph Engineering Co., Ltd., Birmingham Road, Coventry.

Tax: £3 15s per annum (£1 0s. 8d. per quarter).

---

several trials men who were encountered hill-hunting on normal girder fork-equipped machines. Particularly impressive was the sure handling over loose surfaces and greasy grass. Over ruts the "telescopics" helped enormously in absorbing shock and keeping the wheel to the ground, but the impression was gained (and, incidentally, supported by a colleague who later tried the Twin over similar country) that the splendid front end characteristics are a trifle offset by a tendency for the rear wheel to aviate.

It could be that a riding position which brings the weight further rearward would be an advantage—not only on trials type going but also for main road work. Indeed, we would recommend the makers to experiment with footrests at least a full inch further back. This would give a seated position more in keeping with the fast cruising attitude the rider tends to adopt and would help to keep the driving wheel down when "standing on the rests" technique is employed over roughery. Conversely the telescopic forks have effected a very marked improvement on rear-wheel adhesion over fast but bumpy normal road surfaces.

Leaving the West Country via the Cotswold Gate, the next calling point was London and full use was made of the fine, broad road which leads through Northleach and Witney and, of course, of the always tempting Oxford by-pass.

And so in the darkening afternoon the Triumph slipped quietly through London streets, rather mudstained externally, but at heart completely happy and boasting a speedometer collection of miles that included night-work, trials stuff, by-roads, main roads and traffic, not to mention bursts that had reached close on the 80 mark.

Hard Facts

So far, however, the test had been devoted solely to the accumulation of impressions; to garner facts was the next step and, accordingly, stop watches and fuel-measuring containers were sorted out and, in due course, a likely day arrived. As a matter of fact, conditions for speed testing were not perfect (fine, dry, still days are rare at this time of year), for a 10 to 12 m.p.h. wind was blowing obliquely across the selected straight.

Braking was tackled first and several "dummy runs" proved a suspicion which had arisen during ordinary road running. That is that, while excellent stopping results are obtainable, it is not easy to get them without some locking of the rear wheel. This again substantiates our belief that a more rearward riding position would be advantageous. Front wheel braking alone was excellent, although the instant depression of the steering head as the "teles" took up the forward-flung load was somewhat disconcerting at first. However, the front anchor actually held extremely well and the figure of 35 ft. compares most favourably with 37 ft. which was obtained in 1939 with girder forks. Also, the "both brakes" distance of 29 ft. is good, for while it is 1 ft. greater than in 1939, this can be accounted for by the aforementioned tendency of the rear wheel to lock under a relatively light application of the brake.

The next step was to ascertain the maximum speed in the various gears and this was followed by timing from rest to maxima. To round off came the flying quarter. All the results are reproduced in the accompanying graph and test report.

In comparison with 1939 it is true that, generally speaking, throughout the range, the pre-war model was just a shade faster (no more than a mile or two). This is understandable and was expected in view of the lowered com-

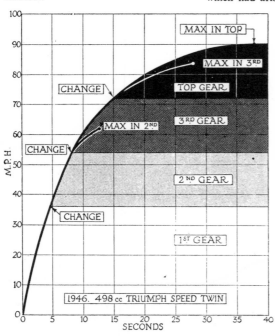

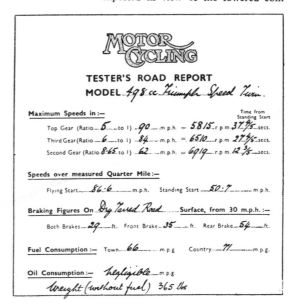

TESTER'S ROAD REPORT

MODEL *498 cc Triumph Speed Twin.*

Maximum Speeds in :—

Top Gear (Ratio *5* to 1) *90* m.p.m. = *5815* r.p.m. *37 4/5* secs.

Third Gear (Ratio *6* to 1) *84* m.p.h. = *6510* r.p.m. *27 4/5* secs.

Second Gear (Ratio *8.65* to 1) *62* m.p.h. = *6919* r.p.m. *12 2/5* secs.

Speeds over measured Quarter Mile :—

Flying Start *86.6* m.p.h.   Standing Start *50.7* m.p.h.

Braking Figures On *Dry Tarred Road* **Surface, from 30 m.p.h. :—**

Both Brakes *29* ft.   Front Brake *35* ft.   Rear Brake *54* ft.

Fuel Consumption :— Town *66* m.p.g.   Country *77* m.p.g.

Oil Consumption :— *Negligible* m.p.g.

Weight (without fuel) 365 lbs.

pression ratio and the current inferior grade of fuel. Nevertheless, the discrepancy is so small that Triumphs are to be congratulated on having achieved so narrow a margin of difference. With No. 1 grade spirit and the compression ratio back at 7¼ there is no reason whatever to doubt that the latest version of the Speed Twin would outpace its forebears.

Out of evil cometh good and the good which cometh out of the evil of " Pool " petrol, so far as the Speed Twin is concerned, is to be found in the really remarkable flexibility which has been achieved. Determined that if he had to give away a shade of speed he would get something back elsewhere, Mr. Turner concentrated on smoother running. The automatic advance and retard device was adopted and, with the " softer " engine characteristics, there results a superbly silken performance which can be dropped right down to 17 m.p.h. on top gear without snatch taking place on full throttle acceleration.

Smooth Power

Throughout the cruising range a turbine-like surge of power is always available and this, to the tester's way of thinking, more than compensates for the disappearance of a mile or so at the end of the speed curve which is seldom used. Docility, sweetness, controlled power, these are three most valuable assets as any high-average rider knows. It is the man who can cover his miles effortlessly who most easily builds up the total and who most enjoys himself, and the Triumph Speed Twin is just the machine to help him do that thing.

But a road test that does nothing but praise fails in its purpose—nothing is perfect and criticism is free. There is, however, not much to criticize adversely about the Speed Twin; its equipment, its finish, its oil-tightness, appearance, performance, general accessibility and handling are all of a very high order.

We have mentioned the footrests, but that may be an individual foible. We did not feel quite happy about our gear changes from second to third; too much effort was required, but that may have been due to an individually awkward box. The only other matter which did not please us was the very retiring position of the carburetter air-slide control. To reach this with a gloved hand on a cold morning was by no means easy. It is true that on almost any ordinary day there is no need whatever to use this control but, on the other hand, rather wasteful flooding of the float chamber is necessary if it is dispensed with. If a twist-grip-controlled air-slide is not feasible (it would retain the clean handlebar ideal) at least the direct control of the carburetter should be made more accessible.

And now the reader is free to browse on the performance figures, the specification and the pictures. In the last-named is to be seen one of the most handsome motorcycles ever produced. With its clean lines and compactness it looks, and is, functionally correct. Can we say more than that it is a motorcycle which the most exacting enthusiast may be proud to own?

ROAD TESTS OF NEW MODELS

349 c.c. TRIUMPH

A High-class Touring Machine Incorpora

IN its general lines the 350 c.c. Triumph 3T follows the renowned 500 c.c. Speed Twin. The side-by-side o.h.v. twin-cylinder engine is an outstanding example of British engineering. It is quiet and docile, yet lively. It is the basis of a machine on which it is a joy to potter and which, at the other end of the scale, can provide high, effortless cruising speed. The 3T can be throttled down to speeds as low as 10-11 m.p.h. in top gear or, if desired, will hum along at 55-60 m.p.h.

Sleek lines—the 3T is attractively finished in black and chromium with white edge-lines

Starting is effortless. No exhaust-valve lifter is fitted; none is needed for kickstarting. Cold or hot, the engine would start at the first light dig on the kickstarter. At no time during the test was the air valve used. It was not required. When the engine was cold, all it was necessary to do as regards carburation was to flood. The model being equipped with automatic advance and retard for the magneto, the handlebar controls are those for the clutch, front brake and throttle.

Idling was at all times exceptionally good. It was so slow that the strokes could almost be counted, yet it was completely reliable. The engine was remarkably quiet. When it was idling there was a gentle rustle from the valve gear. Apart from that, there was merely the quiet hum of well-lubricated machinery. The exhaust, too, was unobtrusive. In fact, so quiet is the 3T that alongside other traffic it is inaudible to the rider, and at speed on the open road the swish from tyres, etc., is louder than either engine or exhaust noises.

Throughout the throttle range the carburation was clean-cut and sweet. This was so even when the engine had only just been started from cold; the air control, it should be repeated, was never used. The pick-up was faultless, and remained so throughout the period of the road test.

The gear change may be classed among the best to-day. The pedal pressure required was commendably light and the travel of the pedal short. Clean, snappy changes could be made between top and third gears, giving added zest to the lively performance of the engine. Changing from bottom gear to second or from second to third called for a slight pause between the

gears. It is not to be implied from this that the gear change was slow. But that slight pause eliminated any chance of the rider making a "scrunch" change. All the indirect gears were inaudible.

The clutch freed perfectly. It was found that when starting from cold it was advisable to free the clutch by use of the kick-starter before attempting to engage bottom gear. That done, there was no sound as bottom gear was engaged, even if the engine was running on the fast side.

The riding position is comfortable for a shorter-than-average rider, but for a taller person a different relationship between saddle and footrests would be appreciated. All the controls are well placed relative to handlebars or footrests, as the case may be. The clutch was light in operation. So, too, were both brake controls; with the ratchet on the Triumph twistgrip new, the throttle could not be operated with the degree of delicacy that is desired by some riders.

Steering and road-holding were of a high order. The Triumph telescopic fork takes care of bumpy surfaces in a satisfactory manner. On very bad road surfaces or at speed, the steering damper was screwed down about a couple of turns, then any chosen line on corners and bends could be held without effort, and straight-ahead steering was perfect. At low speeds there was no trace of rolling and the rider could come to a halt if he wished before dropping his feet from the footrests.

It has already been implied that the 350 c.c. engine is a thoroughly sound engineering job. The 3T was always happy,

The 349 c.c. overhead-valve twin is a neat, compact power unit. It is remarkably quiet, both mechanically and in its exhaust

3T De Luxe

Spring Hub : Flexible Yet Lively

whether being ridden at just above its non-snatch speed or on almost full throttle. Indeed, on one occasion, in company with a much bigger machine, the Triumph covered nearly 90 miles in two hours. Cruising speed on that journey was about 60 m.p.h., and full throttle was used on several occasions. All that was apparent as a result was a slight discolouring of the offside exhaust pipe, and a trace of oil on the rear of the machine.

The engine itself was completely oil-tight. After the machine had covered roughly 400 miles in two days—many of them at speed—not a single trace of oil appeared outside the engine. A wipe over with a rag would restore the Triumph to its pristine showroom condition. But the 3T is as happy in town traffic as it is at speed on the open road. The engine is amazingly tractable, and uttered no protest even when throttled down to speeds as low as 10-11 m.p.h. in top gear.

Timing-case cover and gear-box end are highly polished. The engine proved 100 per cent oil-tight

Braking Figures

It is especially pleasant on the 3T to waft up to a roundabout or corner, round it, and accelerate happily away—still in top gear. That applies at places where second gear would be called for on many modern machines. Acceleration is as brisk as would be expected from any touring-type three-fifty, and at speed the miles are gobbled up in a smooth, vibrationless and fuss-less manner.

Both brakes are light in operation and well up to their job. The braking figure of 26 feet from 30 m.p.h. is a mean of several figures, the poorest of which was 28 feet. No brake adjustment was called for during the period of the road test.

Stability on greasy road surfaces was up to the general high Triumph standard. The prop-stand—a Triumph accessory—fits snugly away out of sight behind the exhaust pipe when raised. However, this makes it rather inaccessible for lowering into use. A rear stand is also fitted and, by use of the side lifting handles, raising the model on to it required no great physical effort or knack, although care was necessary to keep the shins away from the tail pipes. An excellent feature is that the petrol filler cap never allowed any petrol to spill on the tank—even if the tank was filled to maximum capacity.

In one day, in the course of the tests, three heavy thunderstorms were encountered. Such is the adequacy of the mud-guarding and so well protected are the magneto and carburettor that there was no trouble from water.

The initial stiffness in the spring hub had not worn off when the machine was returned to the works. It is known from past experience, however, that the ingenious spring hub is a well-worth-while investment. When fully run in it effects a great improvement in road-holding and general handling, and irons out road irregularities in a satisfactory manner.

The general appearance of the 3T is essentially de luxe; it is a docile yet lively touring three-fifty with an appeal of its own. The finish is black and chromium, with white edge-lines on the tank and white medial lines on the mudguards. The timing-case cover, gear-box end cover and primary-chain case are all highly polished.

Information Panel

349 c.c. Triumph 3T De Luxe

SPECIFICATION

TYPE : Triumph 3T with spring hub.

ENGINE : 349 c.c. (55 x 73.4 mm), vertical-twin o.h.v. Fully enclosed valve gear. High tensile alloy-steel connecting rods with plain big-ends ; mainshaft mounted on ball bearings. Dry-sump lubrication ; oil-tank capacity, 6 pints.

CARBURETTOR : Amal ; Triumph ratchet twistgrip throttle control ; air slide operated by cranked lever on carburettor.

TRANSMISSION : Triumph gear box with positive-stop foot control, Top gear, 5.8 to 1. Third, 6.95 to 1. Second, 10.0 to 1. Bottom, 14.7 to 1. Multi-plate clutch with cork inserts running in oil. Primary chain $\frac{1}{2}$in. x 0.305in. in aluminium oil-bath case. Secondary chain, $\frac{5}{8}$ x $\frac{3}{8}$in. lubricated by bleed from primary case. R.p.m. at 30 m.p.h. in top gear, 2,300 approx.

IGNITION AND LIGHTING : B.T.-H. (or Lucas) magneto with auto-advance. Separate Lucas dynamo. 7in diameter head lamp.

FUEL CAPACITY : $3\frac{1}{8}$ gallons.

TYRES : 19 x 3.25in. Dunlop front and rear.

BRAKES : Triumph $6\frac{7}{8}$ x $1\frac{1}{8}$in. front ; 8 x $1\frac{1}{8}$in rear (with spring hub). Hand adjusters.

SUSPENSION : Triumph telescopic front fork with hydraulic damping. Triumph spring hub in rear wheel.

WHEELBASE : 55in ; ground clearance, 6in unladen.

SADDLE : Terry ; unladen height, 28in.

WEIGHT : 343lb with one gallon of fuel, oil-tank full, and fully equipped.

PRICE : £128 plus Purchase Tax (in Britain)—£162 11s. 3d. Speedometer extra £4, plus £1 1s. 8d P.T. Spring hub extra, £16, plus £4 6s. 5d P.T.

ROAD TAX : £3 15s a year ; £1 0s 8d a quarter.

MAKERS : Triumph Engineering Co., Ltd., Meriden Works, Allesley, Coventry.

DESCRIPTION : *The Motor Cycle*, September 25th, 1947.

PERFORMANCE DATA

MAXIMUM SPEED : First : 36 m.p.h.
Second : 46 m.p.h.
Third : 65 m.p.h.
Top : 68 m.p.h.

ACCELERATION :

	10-30 m.p.h.	20-40 m.p.h.	30-50 m.p.h.
Bottom	$3\frac{3}{5}$ secs.	—	—
Second	$4\frac{4}{5}$ secs.	$5\frac{1}{5}$ secs.	—
Third	8 secs.	$7\frac{1}{5}$ secs.	$7\frac{2}{5}$ secs.
Top	$9\frac{2}{5}$ secs.	$9\frac{2}{5}$ secs.	$9\frac{1}{5}$ secs.

Speed at end of quarter mile from rest : 65 m.p.h.
Time to cover standing quarter-mile : 22 secs.

PETROL CONSUMPTION : At 30 m.p.h., 96 m.p.g. At 40 m.p.h., 81.6 m.p.g. At 50 m.p.h., 70.4 m.p.g. At 60 m.p.h., 65.6 m.p.g.

BRAKING : From 30 m.p.h. to rest, 26ft (surface, dry tar macadam).

TURNING CIRCLE : 15ft 3in.

MINIMUM NON-SNATCH SPEED : 10 m.p.h. in top gear.

WEIGHT PER C.C. : 0.908 lb.

Road Tests of Current Models

JUST over three years ago " Motor Cycling's " first post-war road test was completed, and readers were able to see a pen picture of that pre-war favourite, the Triumph " Speed Twin." At the time of the 1946 test the Triumph was the only vertical twin to be seen on our roads; to-day, if not the only one, it is undoubtedly the most numerous.

The basic specification of the machine is too well known to need more than the accompanying panel to refresh readers' memories, but a host of 1949 improvements are immediately apparent and it is difficult to know quite where to start. Perhaps the most obvious innovation is the new instrument nacelle. Into this are neatly grouped the speedometer and those instruments that were previously contained in a panel on the top of the tank. The unit is in two pieces and encloses head lamp, speedometer. ammeter, lighting switch, cut-out button and horn. Rubber mountings are provided for the instruments, which are internally illuminated, and the head lamp is adjustable at the rim. At the rear of the nacelle protrudes the steering damper knob.

In the Modern Manner

From the sides of the nacelle project the adjustable " new look " handlebars, on to which are clipped only three controls—clutch lever, brake lever and the latest type twist grip; gone is the ratchet fitting and in its place is a grip with finger-controlled friction adjustment. To minimize fraying, the cable passes through a right-angled, chrome-plated tube for the first few inches of its length. The horn button is integral with the handlebar on the left side, the dip switch, on the right, being clipped to the front brake lever.

The Model 5T 498 c.c. o.h.v.
"SPEED TWIN"
TRIUMPH

cleaner, now fitted as standard to all Triumph road machines. Oil-wetted muslin is used for the filtering medium which is easily detachable for cleaning.

One further detail should be mentioned before considering the behaviour of the machine itself. In order to eliminate lengths of small-diameter tubing and to minimize leaks, the oil gauge has been dispensed with and replaced by a simple button indicator located at the base of the timing case cover.

Most of our testing was done in the Midlands, with a part of the mileage over some atrocious urban surfaces, and we soon found that, over tram lines, cobbles and setts the sprung hub absorbed all but the most severe bumps. Over surfaces that would produce daylight between the saddle and the rider of a rigid frame. the Triumph " wafted " easily, taking all the punishment to itself and transmitting

A machine which set a fashion to the motorcycling world. The vertical-engined 498 c.c. "Speed Twin" Triumph here shown with sprung hub in the rear wheel.

Three items additional to the normal specification were fitted to the model tested—a tank-top parcel grid, a prop stand and a sprung hub. Of the first it can be said that here is the very thing for the man who likes to strap waders or leggings to the tank. Normally. after months of such use. signs of this treatment begin to show. Now, with the articles strapped to the grid, the tank top retains its finish.

Swinging forward from a point in front of the nearside footrest, the prop stand is held in position, out or in, by a spring. It is efficient and simple to operate, although its position under the exhaust pipe does necessitate pulling out with the hand; replacement is easier, a push with the foot being sufficient to return the " leg " to its stowed position.

The third extra, the sprung hub, has already been featured in " Motor Cycling," both as a drawing and in written descriptions. Suffice, therefore, to say that the whole unit, enclosed by an alloy shell, adds only 3 per cent. to the total weight of the machine and the wheel moves in an arc (centre-point of which is the gearbox mainshaft) about the stationary spindle in the rear frame members. A single nipple lubricates all moving parts.

Connected to the Amal carburetter by a rubber tube, and located between the battery and the oil tank, is the air

The head lamp nacelle, a 1949 Triumph feature, which materially "cleans-up" the front of the machine and the handlebar assembly.

nothing of shocks or jars to the man in the saddle.

For the first part of the week the weather was fine, but very cold. Nevertheless, on no occasion was there any difficulty in starting the engine; with the float chamber full and the air lever closed, two digs on the kick-starter were sufficient to bring the motor to life. When cold a small

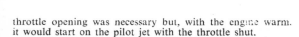
(Right) "Motor Cycling's" Midland man, Dennis Hardwicke, puts the "Speed Twin" through its paces and finds it good.

Impressions of A Firm Favourite "Five Hundred" in 'Forty-nine Form

(Below) The now famous Triumph sprung rear hub, listed at £16 extra, plus P.T. This suspension system has been well tried in racing as well as hard road-riding.

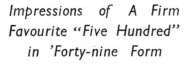

throttle opening was necessary but, with the engine warm, it would start on the pilot jet with the throttle shut.

The riding position is adjustable and can quickly be set to suit personal preference. Handlebars, footrests, footchange lever, footbrake lever and saddle can all be moved up or down. Alterations necessary to suit the tester consisted of lowering the footrests and adjusting foot controls in sympathy. The handlebars fell naturally and comfortably to hand in their standard setting.

No attempt was made to take the Triumph across country. It was felt, apparently in common with the company, who have produced a special machine for the purpose, that trials have become the prerogative of a machine designed to cope with conditions beyond the scope of the ordinary touring model. In these conditions a standard machine is at an unreasonable disadvantage.

Silence !

Main road cruising was effortless. At 55 m.p.h. it was difficult to hear the exhaust note above the wind and an unobtrusive hum was the only indication of an internal combustion engine between one's legs. A slight movement of the body was all that was necessary to negotiate sweeping bends as they came and went. When these were sharper than anticipated the "Speed Twin" could be "laid on its ear" with a feeling of complete confidence.

All main road hills encountered could be ridden easily in top gear, and, in fact, other than for starting, traffic congestion and towns, top gear was the only one necessary. As can be seen from the performance data, acceleration was of a very high order, and in third gear it was only necessary to "heap on the coal" to whistle past baulking traffic with the "70s" showing on the speedometer. Few occasions arose on which the maximum could be used, but the reserve of power was certainly there when it was wanted.

So smooth was the unit that no snatch was felt at 20 m.p.h. in top gear and, provided discretion was used with the throttle, no protest was heard from the engine when returning to the legal maximum in towns. At 30 m.p.h. the motor was turning over happily and it required a very brutal hand to produce pinking when accelerating from this speed, the auto-advance ignition control doing its job very satisfactorily. Of the mileage covered in towns, a considerable portion, especially at the end of the test, was in wet weather. The usual varying and extremely tricky surfaces were met with, but on only one occasion did anything untoward occur.

The cast aluminium oil-bath primary chain case enhances the handsome appearance of this well-finished machine. The engine proved to be commendably oil-tight.

BRIEF SPECIFICATION OF THE 498 c.c. Model 5T TRIUMPH SPEED TWIN

Engine: Vertical twin o.h.v., double high camshaft, 63 mm. bore by 80 mm. stroke; capacity 498 c.c.; compression ratio 7:1; dry sump lubrication; totally enclosed valves with duplex Aero springs; high-tensile aluminium-alloy crankcase; H-section connecting rods in R.R. 56 Hiduminium alloy; crankshaft mounted on heavy-duty ball bearings. B.T.H. magneto with automatic control; Amal carburetter with Triumph patent quick-action twist-grip.

Transmission: Four speeds, foot-operated gearbox; ratios, 5.0, 6.0, 8.65, and 12.7 to 1; primary chain enclosed in streamlined polished aluminium oil-bath; rear chain positively lubricated and provided with protection for both top and bottom runs.

Frame: Brazed-up full cradle; special alloy steel; large-diameter tapered front down-tube; spring-up rear stand; clip-up front stand.

Front Forks: Patent Triumph telescopic, with large movement hydraulically damped; automatically lubricated.

Wheels: Triumph design; laced spokes; Dunlop tyres of 26-in. by 3.25-in. section front and 26-in. by 3.50-in. section rear, with security bolt; 7-in. diameter brakes, finger adjustment front and rear.

Tanks: All-welded steel petrol tank, capacity four gallons, with reserve tap; die-cast metal name plates; quick-opening filler; welded steel oil tank with accessible filters, drain-plug and separate vent, capacity one gallon.

Dimensions: Saddle height 29¼ ins. wheelbase 55 ins., overall length 84 ins.; overall width 28½ ins., ground clearance 6 ins.

Weight: 365 lb.

Finish: Amaranth red cellulose and chrome; cadmium-plated nuts and bolts.

Price: £142 (plus £38 6s. 10d. purchase tax). Total price £180 6s. 10d.

Extras: Speedometer, £4 (purchase tax £1 10s. 8d.), total price £5 1s. 8d.; spring wheel, £16 (purchase tax £4 6s. 5d.), total price £20 6s. 5d.; pillion rests, 16s. (purchase tax 4s. 4d.), total price £1 0s. 4d.; prop stand, £1 5s. (purchase tax 6s. 9d.), total price £1 11s. 9d.; parcel grid £1 5s. (purchase tax 6s. 9d.), total price £1 11s. 9d.

Annual Tax: £3 15s. (£1 0s. 8d. per quarter).

Makers: Triumph Engineering Co., Ltd., Meriden Works, Allesley, Coventry.

In a moment of forgetfulness the throttle was opened too quickly on wood blocks, a mistake which confirmed in the tester's mind the excellent inherent stability of the "Speed Twin," which accommodated itself to such clumsy treatment without so much as a tail twitch.

Gentle braking was also called for at this time and in this respect the machine showed up admirably. Throughout the test the brakes gave confidence at whatever speed they were used. At the upper end of the speed range the application of both hand and foot brake produced the characteristic dip of the telescopic forks and a satisfying hiss from the tyres. The sprung hub was probably largely responsible for the way in which the back wheel stuck to the ground and for the improvement over the 1946 retarding figure of the rear brake. The front brake was just a shade disappointing, however. After an impression of power with the initial pressure on the lever, the ultimate results were not quite up to expectations. Taken generally, however, the "anchors" were good and could be commended on the smooth and progressive way in which they did their job.

Gear changes could be made with certainty, although a little care had to be exercised in order to ensure that they were noiseless in the lower ratios. This did not apply, however, to the change between third and top gears which could be made as fast as the pedal was moved, both up and down. Clutch operation was at all times smooth and light in action without a trace of slip or drag.

Night riding was particularly pleasant, the smoothness of the power unit and the spread of light provided by the head lamp combining to give that feeling of "being on top of the world," which results in fast but safe averages.

It would be almost disappointing, however, to find nothing to criticise and some minor details could be noticed that could be borne in mind for future action. One of these, the position of the prop stand under the exhaust pipe, has already been mentioned. Further small points, the first of which is easily altered, cropped up. The rubber tube from the oil tank breather split and oil mist covered the cut-out and voltage control unit under the saddle. A rubber-bonded canvas tube would obviate this. The speedometer was not too easy to read when the finger was between the fifty and eighty miles per hour figures, it would be an advantage if the head could be tilted back slightly. The particular instrument under review, incidentally, was rather optimistic at maximum speed. Air levers are still necessary, and, while the position of the air control under the saddle is, in the tester's opinion, better than the plunger on the carburetter, it still takes a little getting used to. It is not easy, however, to suggest an alternative position.

Eagle-eyed enthusiasts will have noted the increase in compression ratio and may, on referring to the performance figures, wonder why there is no increase in speed over the 1946 model which had a compression ratio of 6.5 to 1. At the upper end of the range the gain is nullified by the new air cleaner, although an improvement will be noticed in the standing quarter-mile figure.

During the whole period of the test no oil leaks were apparent, other than the oil mist from the split breather tube, and, apart from travel stains collected during a very wet period, the engine and gearbox were as clean at the conclusion of the test as at the beginning.

The Triumph Engineering Co., Ltd., are, indeed, to be congratulated on producing a very worthy successor to the line of high performance twin-cylinder touring machines which have now held the public's favour for more than 12 years.

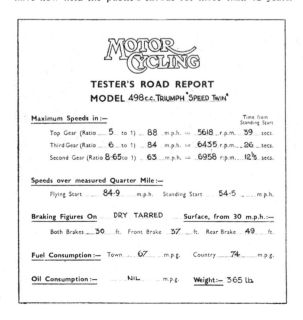

MOTOR CYCLING
TESTER'S ROAD REPORT
MODEL 498 c.c. TRIUMPH "SPEED TWIN"

Maximum Speeds in:— (Time from Standing Start)

Top Gear (Ratio 5 to 1) 88 m.p.h. = 5618 r.p.m. 39 secs.

Third Gear (Ratio 6 to 1) 84 m.p.h. = 6435 r.p.m. 26 secs.

Second Gear (Ratio 8·65 to 1) 63 m.p.h. = 6958 r.p.m. 12⅖ secs.

Speeds over measured Quarter Mile:—

Flying Start 84·9 m.p.h.   Standing Start 54·5 m.p.h.

Braking Figures On DRY TARRED **Surface, from 30 m.p.h.:—**

Both Brakes 30 ft.   Front Brake 37 ft.   Rear Brake 49 ft.

Fuel Consumption:— Town 67 m.p.g.   Country 74 m.p.g.

Oil Consumption:— NIL m.p.g.   **Weight:—** 365 lb

Graph: *1949 498 c.c. TRIUMPH "SPEED TWIN"* — M.P.H. against SECONDS, showing MAX. IN TOP, TOP GEAR, MAX. IN 3RD, CHANGE, 3RD GEAR, MAX. IN 2ND, CHANGE, 2ND GEAR, CHANGE, 1ST GEAR.

A14

ROAD TESTS OF NEW MODELS

498cc Triumph Tiger "100"

A Fast Five-hundred to Appeal to the Sporting Rider

EVEN to-day, ten years after its introduction, the Tiger 100 remains a firm favourite. The engine, the famous 498 c.c. Triumph vertical twin, has become the forerunner of the design that is accepted as the modern trend of the present day. The honour thus accorded the design is well merited, since the machine's high, tireless cruising speed, its outstanding reliability, and its mechanical quietness, have earned the marque a world-wide reputation. The 1949 model under test proved to have all the qualities of its famous forebears—plus a few new ones. It established itself as the fastest five-hundred—and the second fastest machine—to be road tested by *The Motor Cycle* post-war.

There is no doubt that as a machine for high-speed cruising, the Tiger 100 has very few equals either on two wheels or four. Early one Sunday morning, when there was comparatively little traffic abroad, the machine was taken out with the sole object of putting as many miles as possible into each hour. Including two brief halts of about three minutes each, 85 miles were covered in the first 1½ hours — an average speed of over 53 m.p.h.; this, in spite of the fact that on the greater part of the journey speeds in excess of 80 m.p.h. were seldom permissible. The Triumph, in fact, makes British roads seem extra-sinuous, so quickly does one bend follow another. At all times the engine churns out its power with turbine-like smoothness and efficiency. So well subdued is the exhaust and so quiet is the engine that the full performance can be used freely without fear of the machine's passage being the slightest bit obtrusive.

Third Gear Performance

Almost complete silence in the indirect gears is a notable feature. Third gear and top are very close, and, at speeds up to about 40 m.p.h. there was sometimes doubt as to whether third gear or top was in engagement. The performance in third was sparkling in the extreme. From third to top (and *vice versa*) the change was light and instantaneous, so there was a tendency to drop into third at the slightest excuse. Maximum speed available in third gear was 87 m.p.h., and on numerous occasions on normal, fast, main-road runs, the machine was taken up to 80 m.p.h. in third before a snap change was made into top.

The power available was such that on hills the machine would accelerate up to speeds around the 80 m.p.h. mark on gradients that bring many five-hundreds down to 60 m.p.h. There was no marked tendency to pinking.

A first impression, on straddling the Triumph, is that the machine is smaller than a five-hundred. This is because, with its recessed knee-grips, the four-gallon tank is commendably narrow (10in actually) across the knee-grips. The measurement between the hands when the handlebars are gripped is only about 17½ in.

Since the introduction of the instrument nacelle, the sweep of the bars has been altered to bring the grips nearer to the saddle, thus reducing the reach. Saddle height is 29½ in. The relative positions of the saddle, handlebars and footrests combine to give a compact riding position, and one which is well suited to riders of smaller than average stature. For taller riders a higher and slightly more rearward position of the saddle would, no doubt, be appreciated.

Whether the engine was cold or hot, starting was at all times pleasantly easy. After a cold start it was advisable to leave the air slide closed for about two minutes; it could then be opened fractionally and, after, say, a mile had been covered, it could be opened fully. On first acquaintance some difficulty was experienced in operating the air lever placed under the saddle, but later there was no trouble. It was a question of practice. To start the engine when it was hot, it was only necessary to ensure that the throttle

The Triumph front brake is very powerful. Behind the grill under the head lamp glass is mounted the horn

With its silver and chromium finish and trim lines, the Tiger 100 is one of the smartest machines available to-day. The handlebar nacelle houses the head lamp, horn, speedometer, light switch, ammeter, and ignition cut-out button

Cleaned-up handlebars, with the horn button and dip-switch close up to the grips, is a feature of the new model. The tank-top luggage grid is an ingenious and valuable accessory

was closed before "leaning" easily on the kickstarter crank. First-kick starting was as certain as night following day.

Bearing in mind the fact that this is a sports machine, the engine was very quiet mechanically. Even after a cold start there was only a faint mechanical rustle from the valve gear and a trace of piston slap. With the air-filter (which is now standard) in position, there was a complete absence of induction hiss. The air-filter, incidentally, made no appreciable difference to the performance. At low speeds the exhaust was barely audible. The tickover was slow and even, and 100 per cent. reliable.

The clutch was light in operation and took up the drive smoothly and sweetly. Clean, rapid gear changes were possible between third gear and top with hardly any alteration to the throttle opening and only slight easing of the clutch. The pedal movement is light and short. Between first and second, and second and third gears, effortless gear changing could be accomplished by making a slow, gentle movement with the right foot. The Triumph gear change, incidentally, is of the up to change up and down to change down variety. The change was unusually sensitive to spot-on primary and rear chain adjustment.

The engine remained clean externally. Even after 1,000 miles had been covered there were only faint oil smears at the primary-chain case and timing chest joints, and a little oil on the rear wheel rim.

Low-speed pulling was smooth, and only a trace of roughness was apparent—at 20 m.p.h. in top gear. Engine balance was excellent and unimpaired throughout the speed range, except for a very slight vibration period at around 55 m.p.h. in top gear.

Steering, road-holding and braking were fully in keeping with the Tiger 100's sports performance. Corners and bends could be taken effortlessly at speeds round the 70-75 m.p.h. mark without any tendency to chopping or drifting. When bend swinging at speeds over 80 m.p.h. there was slight snaking, even when the steering damper was gripping, but it was never serious enough to be disconcerting. Straight-ahead steering was very good. Only when the road surface was unduly bumpy was there any trace of wheel hop. The spring hub took care of road shocks satisfactorily, but the impression was gained that the fork action could, with advantage, have been lighter round the static load position.

Both brakes were smooth, powerful and progressive in action. For a brief period during the course of the road test the front brake lost some of its efficiency. It had a tendency to fade when used from very high speeds. Inspection revealed nothing at fault, and later, for no apparent reason, the efficiency returned.

With the exception of the clutch lever and twistgrip, which were a shade heavy, the controls were light and smooth in operation.

The tank-top luggage grid proved to be a most useful accessory; during the test there was always *something* on it. Fitted on the bottom frame tube, behind the nearside exhaust pipe, the propstand folded unobtrusively out of sight when not required. However, when set so that it would not foul the road on left-hand corners it could not be lowered by the rider's foot. In its near-horizontal position on the instrument nacelle the speedometer could not be easily read from a normally seated position. The instrument was accurate at 30 m.p.h.; it read 50 m.p.h., at 45; 60 at 54; 70 at 62 and 100 at 90 m.p.h.

The finish is in silver and chromium, and the general appearance is outstandingly trim. In design and workmanship, the Triumph is a sound example of British motor cycle engineering at its best.

Information Panel

SPECIFICATION

ENGINE: 498 c.c. (63 x 80 mm.) vertical-twin o.h.v., fully enclosed valve-gear. Hiduminium alloy connecting rods; plain bearing big-ends; mainshafts mounted on ball bearings. Dry-sump lubrication; oil tank capacity, 6 pints.

CARBURETTOR: Amal; twistgrip throttle control; air slide operated by Bowden cable with lever situated under saddle.

TRANSMISSION: Triumph four-speed gear box with positive-stop foot control. Bottom, 12.7 to 1. Second, 8.65 to 1. Third, 6.0 to 1. Top 5.0 to 1. Multi-plate clutch with cork inserts operating in oil. Primary chain, $\frac{1}{2}$ x 0.305 in. in oil-bath case. Secondary chain, $\frac{5}{8}$ x $\frac{1}{4}$ in. lubricated by bleed from primary chaincase. R.p.m. at 30 m.p.h. in top gear, 1,938.

IGNITION AND LIGHTING: B.T-H. magneto with auto-advance. Separate Lucas dynamo. 7 in diameter head lamp.

FUEL CAPACITY: 4 gallons.

TYRES: Dunlop. Front, 3.25 x 19 in ribbed. Rear, 3.50 x 19 in Universal.

BRAKES: Triumph 6$\frac{1}{4}$ in x 1$\frac{1}{8}$ in front; 8 in x 1$\frac{1}{8}$ in rear; hand adjusters.

SUSPENSION: Triumph telescopic fork with hydraulic damping. Triumph spring hub in rear wheel.

WHEELBASE: 55 in. Ground clearance, 6 in unladen.

SADDLE: Terry; unladen height, 29$\frac{1}{4}$ in.

WEIGHT: 384 lb. with $\frac{1}{2}$ gallon of fuel, full oil-tank, and fully equipped (including pillion seat and footrests and tank-top luggage grid).

PRICE: £152, plus Purchase Tax (in Britain), £42 2s 6d. Speedometer extra, £4, plus £1 1s 8d Purchase Tax. Spring hub extra, £16, plus £4 6s 5d P.T. Pillion equipment, luggage grid, and prop-stand extra.

MAKERS: Triumph Engineering Co., Ltd., Meriden Works, Allesley, Coventry.

DESCRIPTION: *The Motor Cycle*, October 7th, 1948.

PERFORMANCE DATA

MAXIMUM SPEED: First: 43 m.p.h.
Second: 56 m.p.h.
Third: 87 m.p.h.
Top: 93 m.p.h.

ACCELERATION:

	10-30 m.p.h.	20-40 m.p.h.	30-50 m.p.h.
Bottom	2.4 secs.	1.8 secs.	—
Second	3.4 secs.	2.8 secs.	2.6 secs.
Third	—	5.0 secs.	4.6 secs.
Top	—	6.2 secs.	6.6 secs.

Speed at end of quarter-mile from rest: 79.3 m.p.h.
Time to cover standing quarter mile : 16.8 secs.

PETROL CONSUMPTION: At 30 m.p.h., 82 m.p.g. At 40 m.p.h., 77 m.p.g. At 50 m.p.h., 67 m.p.g. At 60 m.p.h., 58 m.p.g.

BRAKING: From 30 m.p.h. to rest, 25 feet (surface, coarse, dry chippings).

TURNING CIRCLE: 14 feet.

MINIMUM NON-SNATCH SPEED: 15 m.p.h.

WEIGHT PER C.C.: 1.05 lb.

Figures given are the means of several runs in opposite directions.

Triumphs Introduce a 650 c.c. Twin!

First Three Production Models Average Over 92 m.p.h. at Montlhéry, then Do a Flying Lap at Over 100 m.p.h.

By GEORGE WILSON

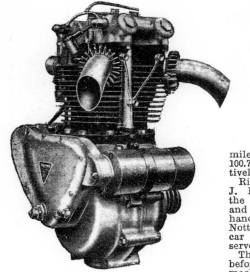

The new 650 c.c. twin develops 34 b.h.p. at 6,000 r.p.m. The design is very similar to that of the Speed Twin engine

A 650 c.c. twin is introduced! A machine designed primarily for sustained high speeds on the vast, smooth highways of America, South Africa and Australia; with an engine developing 34 b.h.p. at 6,000 r.p.m.; and a total weight of little more than that of the famous 500 c.c. Speed Twin. Truly a mount to whet the interest of every enthusiast.

Last week, at the Montlhéry Autodrome near Paris, the first three production models, with full equipment, were subjected to the most severe standard machine test held post-war. The test was entirely successful. The three machines covered 500 miles at an average speed of 92.23, 92.48, and 9..33 m.p.h. respectively. Even taking into consideration stops for re-fuelling, change of riders, and, in one instance, changing a petrol tank which developed a leak, the respective averages were 90.30, 90.93, and 86.07 m.p.h. for the 500 miles. Even more astonishing, at the end of the 500

miles the machines did flying laps at 100.71, 100.71, and 101.78 m.p.h. respectively.

Riding the three were A. Scobie, J. L. Bayliss and S. B. Manns, of the Triumph staff; and Allan Jefferies and P. H. Alves. All arrangements were handled by H. G. Tyrell Smith and Ernie Nott. Harold Taylor, the famous sidecar driver, acted as official A.C.U. observer.

The test actually began a couple days before the Montlhéry "show," when the machines, fitted with panniers, set out from the works at Coventry. They were ridden through London en route to Folkestone, and, on landing in France, they were ridden again to Montlhéry. After the machines had been stripped of their panniers, they were given a preliminary run round the track, checked over, and the test embarked upon.

For the purpose of the test, several slight departures from production standard were made. For example, out of consideration of safety for the riders (and on Dunlop's advice) racing tyres were fitted. So that the riders could adopt the racing crouch comfortably, racing-type mudguard pads, small Trophy-model saddles, and fixed rearward footrests were used. Because of the position of the offside footrest, it was not, unfortunately, possible to use the kick-starter, so push starts were employed. Again because of the safety factor (an incandescent plug can easily lock an engine), K.L.G. racing plugs were fitted. Whereas the standard size main jet on the production job is 190, 210 jets were used in the test. Also, because the horn bracket on one of the

machines had fractured in practice, the horns were removed from all three machines. Extra strong clutch springs were fitted, and 25-tooth engine sprockets which will probably be standard for oversea, were used (24-tooth sprockets will be fitted on machines for the home market). Compression ratios were 7 to 1, as standard, and the fuel used was 72-octane Pool quality.

The Montlhéry track is concrete surfaced and very bumpy on the bottom curve. It measures 1.583 miles per lap and has steeply banked curves at each end. The track has immense width, so much so that when you take a machine round for the first time you hardly know where to point it! Because of the bump at the bottom, circling the track at speed is a job that is arduous in the extreme for both rider and machine.

A 95 m.p.h. Lap

On the morning of the day scheduled for the test, the track lay under a grey, cloudy sky dotted with blobs of blue. When the machines arrived, a capricious racing mount with a megaphone exhaust system was being patiently prepared for a record attempt. Work on the "freak" machine continued throughout the day; the job never performed satisfactorily, in marked contrast to the standard Triumphs, which from the word "go" gave of their best and kept on doing so quietly and without fuss!

Promptly at 9 a.m., Scobie set off on the No. 1 machine to complete a couple of warming-up laps before beginning the test proper. At 9.15 the actual test was on. Scobie was pushed off and got

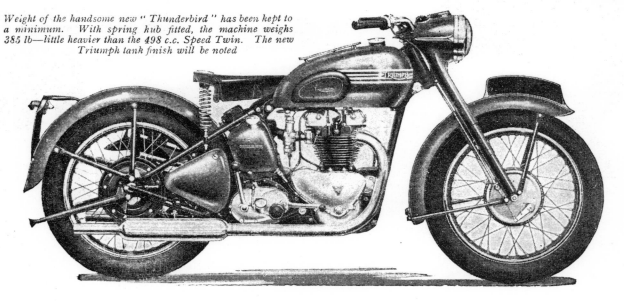

Weight of the handsome new " Thunderbird " has been kept to a minimum. With spring hub fitted, the machine weighs 385 lb—little heavier than the 498 c.c. Speed Twin. The new Triumph tank finish will be noted

flat down to it right away. His first flying lap took him only 67s (85 m.p.h.). His next lap took 61, and the next 60s dead—a speed of 95 m.p.h. He was immediately given the signal to slow the pace!

At 9.21 a.m. Manns set off on No. 2 machine on his warming-up lap. Scobie had settled down to regular lappery at a speed of slightly over 93 m.p.h. Alves began his preliminary lap at twenty minutes to 10. The sun had now risen and was rapidly gaining strength. When Alves began serious batting, Scobie and Manns were lapping in easy, regular style and were separated by slightly less than the length of the straight. So quiet were the machines that they were inaudible when they were on the far side of the track. The zestful Scobie began to turn up the wick again and overhauled Manns. Again he was given the "S," and when he cut out the fireworks he was given the O.K.

The first hour passed. There was a certain tenseness at the pits. Would standard, equipped machines maintain this cracking speed? Nothing untoward occurred; each machine lapped with the utmost consistency.

"S" for Jefferies

When Scobie came in at the end of his tour, the tyres were cool and bore little signs of wear, though 66 laps had been covered at an average speed of 91.95 m.p.h. He reported that the most difficult part of the job was keeping the speed down! The engine was absolutely oil-tight; the only external oil seen was on the silencers—where it was being blown from the primary chaincase breather which is used on Triumphs to lubricate the rear chain. The pit stop was very brief; petrol and oil tanks were topped up. Bayliss set off, and Scobie rested.

No. 2 machine came in after the first hour looking as quondam as its sister job. It had covered 63 laps at an average speed of over 92 m.p.h.

Alves was lapping in 62.8s (about 91 m.p.h.), which was considered too slow and he was given the "F" sign.

Jefferies was flat on the tank and riding in too spirited a fashion. He was given "S."

So regularly did the three machines lap that watching them became monotonous. They circled hour after hour with clocklike precision. By then it seemed impossible that anything could possibly go wrong. But something did go wrong! Bayliss pulled into the pits at one o'clock on No. 3 machine with a split tank. Quickly the tank was removed and one from the spare machine fitted, the whole job taking 15 minutes. Bayliss set off again and settled down at once. The sun rose higher and higher above the clouds. The day became unbearably hot—and still the machines carried on. Stops for refuelling and change of riders came and went. If the machines were being overworked, they showed no sign of it.

At 2.20 p.m., No. 1 machine had completed five hours at an average speed, including stops, of 90.30 m.p.h. The monotony of watching this supreme example of sheer reliability was broken momentarily when Allan Jefferies came in on the bogey No. 3 machine to report that there was a high-pitched scream from the rear chain. All that was wrong, however, was that the bottom run of the rear chain guard was adrift. Quickly it was removed, and Jefferies set off again after a stop lasting about three minutes.

At the end of each machine's 500 miles there was still negligble external oil on the engines. Exhaust pipes, in fact, were only slightly discoloured near the port. Lights were still working on two of the machines, but had ceased to do so on the third; on that one also the ammeter needle had come away from its pivot. Rear chains were badly stretched; primary chains and tappets required no adjustment whatever.

When the machines had been checked and the rear chains adjusted, they each did a flying lap flat-out and achieved the speeds quoted earlier. I could not then resist having a whang on one of the machines, but because a free track was impatiently awaited by a French driver with a blown racing car, I

Allan Jefferies takes the "Thunderbird" round Montlhéry track at a speed around the century mark

got only three laps in before being flagged off.

The 650 c.c. Twin—to be called the Thunderbird, incidentally—is a man's machine if ever there was one. On my first circuit round the track I could not use full bore—this on a track four times as wide as the widest main road and with almost sheer banking on the curves —so phenomenal is the performance. On the second circuit I was clocking 100 m.p.h. on the straight past the pits, but again rolled the grip back when encountering the bump on the lower curve. Even on the third lap, I tended to shut off slightly, although I was getting the feel of things with each tour.

The engine felt to be working no harder at 100 m.p.h. than my own Speed Twin engine is at 75-80. Acceleration is far and away superior to that of any five-hundred and is definitely of the racer variety. Low-speed torque was not so good as I had expected,

The three Triumphs, after completing the 500 miles, covered a flying lap. Riders are, left to right, S. B. Manns, L. J. Bayliss, and A. Scobie

TRIUMPHS INTRODUCE
——A 650 c.c. TWIN——

but, of course, with the machine's 25-tooth engine sprocket, the gearing was higher than that to which I am accustomed.

What of the new model's technical features? The Thunderbird design is based on that of the long-established Speed Twin—forerunner of every other vertical-twin in production to-day. Bore and stroke of the engine are 71×82mm, as against 63×80mm for the five-hundred. Graphs showing the power curves of the new engine and the Speed Twin reveal that the Thunderbird engine develops the same b.h.p. at 4,000 r.p.m. as the Speed Twin does at 6,000. At 6,000 r.p.m., the 650 c.c. engine is producing 34 b.h.p. on a 7 to 1 compression ratio: 7½ more h.p. than the Speed Twin at similar engine speed.

However, the full advantage of the larger capacity engine is not to be found in sheer h.p. at high r.p.m. alone. The power curve is "flat," and the torque at low revolutions per minute—in fact, at all revs.—is vastly superior to that of the Speed Twin.

Stronger Con-rods

With true Triumph ingenuity the weight has been kept to a bare minimum. Indeed, the difference in weight between the Thunderbird and the Speed Twin is no more than a pound or two. The approximate weight is 365lb or, with the spring hub, which is an optional fitting, 385lb. Thus we have a fully equipped six-fifty with rear-springing delivering 34 b.h.p. and tipping the scales at 385lb; a 650 c.c. retaining all the handling attributes of a British five-hundred and possessing the high, effortless cruising speed of the 700lb or so machines popular in the U.S.

Though inertia stresses in the new engine are likely to be less than those of the 500 c.c. twin, power for power—as given power is achieved at lower revs—stronger connecting rods are fitted.

These are light-alloy, H-section stampings in RR56, and are almost identical in design with the rods used in the Grand Prix engines. The lower half of the big end eye is a white-metal-lined steel forging, and the unit is held together by a pair of 100-ton tensile strength nickel-chrome big-end bolts. In journal diameter and proportion the crankshaft is of the same dimensions as that of the five-hundreds, but, of course, the throw is increased by 1mm to give the 82mm stroke.

The cylinder head and barrel are almost identical in appearance with those of the Speed Twin. In fact, a casual glance reveals virtually no difference.

Sufficient Power

Efficient combustion chamber design is cleverly achieved. Valve geometry is not decided, as is usual, by the machined hemispheres of the combustion chambers. Instead, each valve has its own supplementary hemisphere machined about the valve seat. The advantage of this is increased compression ratio without resort to an exaggerated dome on the piston. Thus the weight of the piston is kept down and an efficient combustion chamber is achieved.

A Tiger "100"-type Amal carburettor with a choke diameter of 1in is fitted. The induction manifold in the head conforms to Speed Twin practice except that it has larger-cored passages. It was explained by Mr. Edward Turner that the fitting of an even larger carburettor gives increased top-end power, but that there is so much power available that this is not only unnecessary, but undesirable! Valves measure 1 7⁄16in across the seat—an increase of ⅛in over those of the Speed Twin. Rockers, push-rods, tappets and cams are identical with those of the Speed Twin, and there is no deviation from Speed Twin valve or ignition timing.

Originally, on the Speed Twin, rocker-gear oil draining was by means of external pipes which led the oil down to the push-rod tubes. In later models these oil drains were drilled in the cylin-

der, thus obviating the need for external oil pipes. The original draining scheme has been reverted to in the 650 c.c. engine since, with the larger bores, there is insufficient metal to accommodate drilled oilways.

Apart from these differences, the remainder of the engine is identical with that of the Speed Twin. Six-fifty and five-hundred timing gear is interchangeable, and the crankcases are virtually identical as regards appearance. The oil-pump of the 650 c.c. engine, however, has increased capacity, circulating some 25 per cent more oil.

In order to cope with increased b.h.p., the transmission has been slightly modified. An extra plate has been added to the clutch, making a total of five plates. The gear box itself has been redesigned and opportunity has been taken in the redesigning to provide easier engagement from 1st to 2nd and from 2nd to 3rd gears. This has been achieved by re-

A cutaway illustration of the ingenious Triumph spring hub, which is an optional extra on the Thunderbird

lieving alternate dogs. The 24-T. sprocket gives top, 4.57; third, 5.46; second, 7.75; bottom, 11.2 to 1. A further change in the gear box is the provision for an integral speedometer drive. The cable now emerges horizontally from the gear box on the timing side of the machine, and allows the cable to pass up to the speedometer head in an easy sweep.

Triumphs have decided, on the score of reliability, not to chromium-plate tanks in future. It has been found, as was pointed out in a Leader in *The Motor Cycle*, that particularly in the case of machines sent oversea, trouble has been experienced with rust, the deposit of which is encouraged by the combination of the plating process and the consequent sea-crossing. It has also been ascertained that chromium plating tends to weaken the welded seams. The Thunderbird tank is therefore finished in an attractive shade of grey-blue, and there is a tank motif in the form of a chromium-plated band on which is mounted the badge.

Steering geometry, frame proportion, wheelbase, brakes, saddle height, and riding position are identical with those of the Speed Twin. The handlebar nacelle is, of course, being retained. Tank-top parcel grids, because of their popularity, have been standardized on Thunderbird models; the speedometer, also, is included in the purchase price.

What of a production date? The first of the new models should be leaving the factory during the second week in October. Although the initial production will go oversea, it is anticipated that a good proportion will be made available for riders at home before Christmas. The price is £153, plus Purchase Tax (in Great Britain only), £41 6s 3d, making a total of £194 6s 3d, without spring hub, but including speedometer and parcel grid. The spring hub costs £16 (plus P.T. £4 6s 5d). The makers are the Triumph Engineering Co., Ltd., Meriden Works, Allesley, Nr. Coventry, England.

Good show : Mr. Edward Turner, managing director, Triumphs, congratulates all concerned immediately after the arduous test

Road Tests of Current Models—

THE Triumph 650 c.c. "Thunderbird" was introduced to the public, just prior to the Earls Court Show in 1949, by means of a remarkable high-speed demonstration at the Montlhéry track, near Paris, in which three production models each covered 500 miles at a speed in excess of 92 m.p.h., with a final flying lap of 100.71 in two cases and 101.78 in the other. Since then innumerable requests for a "Motor Cycling" road test report have been received from readers, requests which we are now able to satisfy.

Following an established tradition— the "Speed Twin" Triumph was the first of the modern popular vertical twin-engined motorcycles—the "Thunderbird" was the first of the larger capacity engines of this type to be announced and has proved as popular and as successful as the earlier 500 c.c. model.

With an increased power output—well over 30 b.h.p. is available—and without any additional weight, the performance of the newcomer was rightly anticipated to be something rather exceptional. Vital to the maintenance of high average speed is the ability to cruise in excess of 70 m.p.h. without in any way "fussing" the engine and, indeed, cruising as such is dependent on weather conditions and the stamina of the rider rather than the speed at which the "Thunderbird" will travel. No difficulty was experienced in keeping the speedometer needle above the 80 m.p.h. mark and on one road, frequently travelled, the average speeds were high enough to produce a firm resolve that, other than in the company of close friends, no mention of them would be made.

Continued use over roads "not so good" and frequently only "just fair" has borne out an early impression that, from point to point, this is one of the *really* quick motorcycles. Speed alone does not produce this impression. It is built up from the satisfactory working of every component on the machine and

The 650 c.c. o.h.v. Model 6T
VERTICAL TWIN
TRIUMPH
"THUNDERBIRD"

"Motor Cycling" Describes the Road Behaviour of the Biggest Machine in the Range—with a Three-figure Maximum Speed

(Above, right) A near-side view of the 650 c.c. power unit. With a bore and stroke of 71 mm. × 82 mm. it develops 34 b.h.p. at 6,300 r.p.m. (Below) The "Thunderbird" looks what it is—a fast but tractable machine capable of "hitting the hundred." The "Twin-Seat," is an extra.

(Above) The "Thunderbird" on the road. On test it was found to be readily responsive to throttle and brakes and so easy to handle as to maintain a high standard of safety.

(Left) The ingenious Triumph sprung rear hub, with which the "Thunderbird" tested was equipped. It provides an excellent degree of comfort and materially aids the road-holding qualities of the machine.

finally from an indeterminable feeling that, come tractor or motor coach on the narrowest of roads, all will be well. Of the tangible things, consider first the riding position. Admirable in all respects, the "Twin-Seat" accommodates itself to any riding position adopted, sitting up and pottering, or head down and banging along a good arterial road. Footrests are adjustable to three positions, long, medium or short, and both the long and the short rider will find them equally comfortable. Any relative position can be chosen for foot brake

On the left is shown the distinctive headlamp nacelle—a now familiar feature of all Triumphs, in which is housed switchgear, ammeter, cut-out button, concealed horn and speedometer. The tanktop luggage grid is also shown.

or foot change pedals; both are fully adjustable and it is simple to put them where only the slightest movement of the foot is sufficient to produce results. Handlebars are unusual in shape but comfortable in operation and strictly functional in their absence of unnecessary knobs and levers. The automatic advance unit on the magneto makes it possible to dispense entirely with an ignition control, and the air lever has been relegated to a semi-concealed position beneath the saddle. This control does not, in road test parlance, "fall readily to hand," but the knack in using it is soon acquired. Horn button and dip switch are unobtrusive; the former is screwed into the handlebar and the latter is neatly screwed to the rear of the front brake lever clip.

Starting the engine when cold required a little more energy than is normal with vertical twins of 500 c.c.s, but as each cylinder has a capacity of 325 c.c.s it was nothing to cavil at. With the air lever closed and the carburetter flooded slightly, two or three firm prods were all that were necessary to produce the required result. When warm, air control and flooding could be ignored. It was found advisable to keep the air lever nearly closed until the engine really warmed up, but as the carburation proved quite clean from pilot jet to maximum throttle, this was more an indication of "spot on" tuning than of mixture weakness.

Provided the clutch was freed before starting the engine, bottom gear could be selected without noise. Clutch withdrawal was "two finger," and could almost be described at "little finger." Engagement was similarly smooth and the relatively high bottom gear of 11.2 to 1 unnoticeable in consequence. The words "smooth" and "easily" describe the operation of every control. Gear changes could be whipped in up or down, although unless they were made very quickly or very deliberately, changes between second and third produced some slight sign of engagement.

It is difficult to describe the sense of ease felt when cracking along narrow and bumpy roads. From a fast left-hander the machine could be picked up and then banked without conscious effort for a swerve in the opposite direction. The spring wheel must take full credit for its share in the proceedings; although its travel is, theoretically, not designed to cope with potholes of the 4-in. variety, it knocks the bump out of anything less than the 6-in. crater. In addition, it does an excellent job by maintaining the back wheel in contact with the road.

At the bows, the telescopic forks co-operated to full effect and, with more movement available, literally damped out all road shocks. The synchronized suspension ensured complete controllability and, to borrow another well-worn phrase, the test machine "steered to the proverbial hair."

With such excellent road-holding, it is not surprising that the brakes proved

BRIEF SPECIFICATION OF THE 650 c.c. TRIUMPH "THUNDERBIRD"

Engine: Vertical twin-cylinder; bore 71 mm., stroke 82 mm.; 649 c.c.; push-rod o.h.v.; light-alloy connecting rods, plain big ends; dry sump lubrication, oil tank capacity 5 pints; Lucas magneto ignition with automatic advance and retard; Lucas 60-watt dynamo; Amal carburetter.

Transmission: Triumph gearbox; primary chain ½ by 0.305 in.; ⅜ by ⅝ in. final drive chain; positive-stop four-speed gearbox, ratios 4.57, 5.45, 7.75 and 11.2 to 1.

Frame: Cradle frame with Triumph spring wheel; hydraulically controlled telescopic front forks; rear stand and centre prop stand.

Wheels: Fitted with Dunlop tyres. 3.25 by 19-in. ribbed front and 3.50 by 19-in. Universal rear; 7-in. front and 8-in. rear brakes.

Tank: Welded steel fuel tank, capacity 4 gallons; built-in knee grips.

Dimensions: Saddle height, 31½ ins.; wheel base. 55 ins.; ground clearance, 6 ins.; weight, 385 lb.

Finish: Polychromatic "Thunderbird" blue.

Equipment: Lucas lighting with 6-in. head lamp, electric horn, speedometer.

Price: £153 plus £41 6s. 3d. P.T. = £194 6s. 3d. Spring hub £16. plus £4 6s. 5d. P.T. = £20 6s. 5d. Twin-Seat, £1 11s. plus 9s. 6d. P.T. = £2 4s. 6d.

Maker: Triumph Engineering Co., Ltd., Meriden Works, Allesley, Coventry.

---

efficient; even inefficient units would have produced passable results with the wheels so firmly in contact with the ground. And Triumph brakes are by no means inefficient! The 7-in. front brake, with its new cast-iron drum, gave smooth and steady retardation from any speed, and during the test showed signs of "fade" on only one occasion. This occurred during a run down from the highest point of the second highest road in the country, on which occasion the front brake only was used. Assistance from the rear unit on the last hairpin removed any possibility of trouble and, indeed, had both brakes been used properly the fading would never have occurred. The test-panel figures do not give a true impression of braking throughout the speed range and it must be added that in normal use the machine stopped quickly in any circumstance.

Throughout, the engine was unobtrusive, giving its power without noise or fuss. Within the range of revolutions normally used there was no perceptible vibration. For the last 500 r.p.m. available in each gear, some vibration was transmitted through the handlebars, but as more acceleration is available by changing gear before the peak figure is reached, it is probable that it will only be felt when accidentally over-revving or by intentional misuse. Acceleration is, of course, outstanding. From a standstill, 80 m.p.h. is available in just 15 seconds: sufficient to laugh off all but a few other road

users. Outstanding also is the manner in which the speedometer needle surges on from 60 m.p.h. when the twist-grip is turned. On hills, a drop to third gear will give acceleration envied by most on a flat road, or even downhill!

At the other end of the revolution range, it is, perhaps, inevitable that smoothness should suffer slightly. It is unreasonable to expect two 325 c.c. cylinders to be as inconspicuous as those of a 500 c.c. twin. In fact, the difference is very slight, and it is only in top gear, below 25 m.p.h., that the power impulses are noticed.

In order to ensure a full and uninterrupted run when establishing maximum-speed figures, the "Thunderbird" made its timed runs at Montlhéry track. Apart from the difficulty in finding in this country a stretch of road long, straight and flat enough to establish without doubt the absolute maximum of so potent a model, it was the intention to ascertain how closely the performance approached that of the original trio of "Thunderbirds" tried out on that circuit. That 100 m.p.h. was recorded indicates a very high standard of maintained production efficiency in the factory.

It is always satisfying to one's ego to be able to ride to a Halt sign, stop the machine and leisurely touch ground with the feet. In this respect, the Triumph was a shameless flatterer. Without effort, and certainly without any trick balancing, this could be done

time and time again. Very satisfying it was, too, to be in a position to trickle gently up to traffic lights and, without undue noise, be away comfortably in front of the next man. Moreover, exhaust noise was most unobtrusive.

After initial adjustment, the headlight illuminated the road satisfactorily enough to permit cruising speeds up to 65 m.p.h. In the dipped position, easily selected by the very convenient switch, no offence was caused even to that touchy individual, the long-distance lorry driver.

After a considerable mileage, the engine and gearbox remained oil-tight. During the severe driving necessary to obtain figures for the test panel and acceleration graph, some oil was thrown from the chain on to the rear tyre, but overfilling was probably responsible for the oil which frothed out of the filler-cap vent hole on that occasion. It must be emphasized that nothing of this nature occurred during the normal road mileage covered. Also, after the acceleration test, the ammeter insisted on showing an 8 amps. charge, and it is possible the voltage-control unit may have become a trifle deranged during the full-bore runs.

Small criticisms, these, and ones never likely to perturb the average owner. Small enough, certainly, when the overall efficiency, practicability and appearance of the "Thunderbird" are arrayed on the credit side of the ledger.

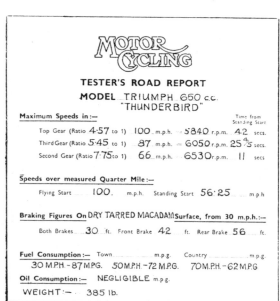

TESTER'S ROAD REPORT

MODEL TRIUMPH 650 c.c. "THUNDERBIRD"

Maximum Speeds in :—

					Time from Standing Start
Top Gear (Ratio 4·57 to 1)	100 m.p.h. = 5840 r.p.m.	42 secs.
Third Gear (Ratio 5·45 to 1)	87 m.p.h. = 6050 r.p.m.	25⅘ secs.
Second Gear (Ratio 7·75 to 1)	66 m.p.h. = 6530 r.p.m.	11 secs.

Speeds over measured Quarter Mile :—

Flying Start 100 m.p.h.   Standing Start 56·25 m.p.h.

Braking Figures On DRY TARRED MACADAM Surface, from 30 m.p.h. :—

Both Brakes 30 ft.   Front Brake 42 ft.   Rear Brake 56 ft.

Fuel Consumption :— Town   m.p.g.   Country   m.p.g.

30 M.P.H.—87 M.P.G.   50 M.P.H.—72 M.P.G.   70 M.P.H.—62 M.P.G.

Oil Consumption :— NEGLIGIBLE m.p.g.

WEIGHT :— 385 lb.

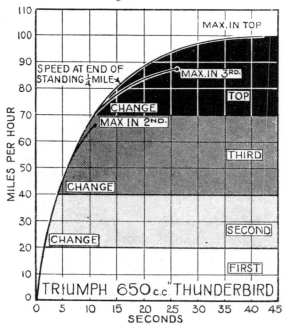

TRIUMPH 650 c.c. "THUNDERBIRD"

Workshop and Open Road : Part 783

Utility Specification?

"TORRENS" Suggests that Many Might Like an Unembellished, Three-speed, 350 c.c. Twin with a Lively Performance

" Torrens " trying the very light, three-speed, 350 c.c. Triumph vertical twin in 1941

A MANUFACTURER who makes more of the components of his motor cycles than is, perhaps, customary remarked a short time ago that he saw no means whereby any substantial cut could be made in the prices of his machines. One might, he said, devise some cheaper method of construction, but the saving would be of little consequence to the purchaser. Even if the entire cost of the machining carried out at his works could be eliminated, the reduction in price, he added, would not be vast.

These statements sent my thoughts coursing back to two articles written during the war. The first was a description of a very light, three-speed, 350 c.c. vertical twin which, if the then Triumph factory had not been razed to the ground, would almost certainly have been standardized for Army use. The second article gave for the first time details of the Civvy Street, four-speed, 350 c.c. Triumph vertical twin which had been due for announcement the very week that war broke out.

Following the first article, with its description of the light, lively three-speed model, there were many letters from readers which said, in effect, " That's the machine for me when I get back home—just that. Please, whatever you do, don't alter it and allow it to grow up." Readers were thrilled at the specification and by the particulars of the machine's performance—rightly so according to my experience with two of the prototypes.

There was a marked change, however, after, tongue in cheek, I had written the second article. This was entitled, " Which Do You Prefer?" and contrasted the simple, light three-fifty designed for Army use with the colourful, four-speed, chromium-plated mount whose announcement had had to be withdrawn from our issue for 7 September, 1939. Allegiance

was immediately transferred to the lustrous model.

Of course, that was wartime, and everyone was sick of olive paint, khaki and drabness. Life as a whole was sombre. It was, I consider, inevitable that, notwithstanding the added cost, everyone should plump for the mount which radiated peace and plenty. Has the pendulum now swung back a little? Would the 230lb, 75 m.p.h. machine, with its excellent power-to-weight ratio, have an appeal today? If so, at what price could it be marketed? Possibly you remember that, when it was originally described, Edward Turner stated that it would cost less to make than the then 350 c.c. single-cylinder, side-valve W.D. Triumph.

Savings Effected

Let us run through features of the specification and note what was shorn off and where savings were effected. First, the tank was part of the frame. Secondly, the engine-gear unit employed a fixed-centre, slipper-adjusted duplex primary chain and provided three gear ratios instead of the nowadays customary four. Thirdly, there was direct lighting from an A.C. generator mounted on the engine shaft. Fourthly, there was a two-into-one exhaust system. Fifthly, there was no spit-and-polish.

For donkey's years, motor cycles had, at the most, three gears. Engines were more flexible then; today, with four gears, designers do not have to worry overmuch. This three-fifty twin in its final form, in which it had plenty of flywheel effect and a small carburettor choke, was an extremely flexible machine; also, I repeat, with its low weight it had an outstandingly good power-to-weight ratio. The machine accelerated in top gear from 20 m.p.h. to 50 m.p.h. in 12.6

secs. As for the tyre size, this was 3.25 × 19in and therefore entirely adequate.

Of course, the machine did not have one of those expensive and, usually, weight-adding extras, a spring frame. And, a criticism as regards its use today, the machine had no battery for parking lamps or for operating an electric horn. Of course, many two-strokes haven't, either. My 125 c.c. W.D.-type Royal Enfield also has simple direct lighting, and what a blessing it is the way I can leave it lying by without having to worry about a battery, knowing all the time that the machine is ready automatically for any night trip.

I feel that, with purses containing more moths than coin, there may be many who would like a three-fifty solo on the lines postulated. It could be colourful without any chromium: After all, standard Triumph tanks are nowadays enamelled, not chromium plated. Thanks to the light weight, the machine would give a most exhilarating performance. Would there not be just about all the average man needed?

Of course, the basic question is: " At what price could the machine be marketed?" Perhaps Mr. Turner would cost the design roughly, taking present-day figures. Certainly a useful amount would be saved as a result of the low weight and, therefore, reduced quantity of material. The simple lighting set would be much, much cheaper than the dynamo, battery, voltage-control unit, etc., of the contrasting design. The smaller brakes mean savings (they have to cope with only a light machine). Something, too, would be saved as a result of the methods of construction, and from the elimination of most of that always expensive item, polishing.

I am not seeking to thrust cheapness down people's throats, but wish solely to suggest that possibly now is a good time to think over the twin questions, " What do I want?" and, " How much can I afford?" My feeling is that motor cycles have tended to become needlessly luxurious and expensive, and that it might be a good thing to get back to simplicity and low weight, especially as every added pound imposes a stranglehold on performance.

" . . . there may be many who would like a three-fifty solo on the lines postulated "

The 498 c.c. TRW

EDWARD TURNER, Triumph Designer and Managing Director, R

By GE

WHY a twin? Why side-by-side valves? Why light-alloy cylinders? Why a pinch-bolt type of crankshaft? The engine of the TRW Military Triumph twin forms an intriguing subject for discussion. The present power unit, it will be recalled, was announced in September, 1948, as that employed to power the standard motor cycle for the Services. The machine was dubbed the Hybrid, because it was a compromise between the ideal and what could be afforded by a stringent peacetime economy. An engine with a host of unusual features, it is a design by Edward Turner, designer and managing director of Triumphs.

I led off by asking him: "The TRW was designed, I know, to comply with a Ministry of Supply specification. But can you tell me why a side-valve twin was chosen rather than its o.h.v. counterpart? What factors, indeed, were there that loaded the scales against the single, bearing in mind that the engine was envisaged for Services work and for production in time of war. The single would be simpler to produce, and thus less costly, and it would be efficient enough. I realize, of course, that with the twin, inertia forces are less because the piston speed is lower, hence bearing stresses are lighter, and longevity is improved."

Reasons for Side Valves

Answer: "The side-valve twin was selected for the following reasons: it was favoured rather than its o.h.v. counterpart since, designed in the light of modern knowledge, an engine of this type is capable of all the performance required for Services work. Because of its simplicity, it presents no great servicing or repair problems to the sometimes relatively unskilled Services personnel who may deal with it. Also, of course, fewer spare parts need be stocked by the various field units.

"A twin was preferred to a single because, on the whole, a twin is more reliable. It is more tractable at low speeds. It is simpler to drive, especially where novices are concerned. Because of its good low-speed torque, less gear changing is required. A twin is kinder to the transmission than is a single and, since there are lower peak loads on the essential bearings, engine longevity must be superior to that of a single. Finally, the only reason this engine is not a four is the high cost of the four."

Question: "If long engine life was one of the aims behind the design, I should have thought that a flat twin would have been better than a vertical twin, if only because, in the flat twin, the inertia masses cancel each other out. Is it not true that the nearer an engine is to having perfect dynamic balance, the longer will be its life?"

Answer: "You are wrong in supposing that a flat twin would outlast the vertical twin. The contrary is, in fact, the case. In order to keep a flat twin within reasonable overall length, valve guides, connecting rods and pistons have to be shorter than ideal engineering considerations demand. No such limitations are placed on a vertical twin. Although the inertia forces do oppose one another in a flat-twin design, there is a pronounced couple which subjects the crankshaft to high bending loads—loads which make it necessary to employ more robust bearings than those normally used. The out-of-balance forces of a vertical twin are easily coped with; when the engine is mounted conventionally in a motor cycle frame, they are reduced to proportions which cause no discomfort to the rider."

Question: "I note that the cylinder block is a light-alloy casting. What is the reason for the use of light alloy?"

Answer: "The first reason is weight reduction. Obviously, there is a considerable saving in this respect over a cast-iron block. The second is that light alloys have better heat conductivity than cast iron."

Question: "In this engine, the cylinders are cast in a single block and both heads are also cast integrally. But it is maintained in some quarters that separate cylinders and heads provide better cooling and greater freedom from distortion, since the mass of metal around the bores can be kept more uniform. May I have your views, please?"

Answer: "Triumph twin-cylinder barrels and heads are cast in integral pairs because excellent rigidity and ease of manufacture result. For instance, both bores and faces are machined at one setting—which is something that could not possibly be achieved if the cylinders were cast separately. No pair of cylinders cast separately can be given ideal symmetry of fin area and metal section because, obviously, of the lack of space between the cylinders. In an integral casting such as ours, the metal mass of one cylinder acts as a heat reservoir for its opposite number. Thus, heat equilibrium is maintained in both cylinders. It follows that in a well-designed en bloc cylinder or cylinder-head casting, there should be less distortion than there is with individual cylinders. Careful design—suitable fin shape and proportion—compensates for uneven section. This is a fact clearly borne out in practice."

Question: "I believe that a disadvantage of light-alloy cylinders in small sizes is that lower thermal efficiency results because of heat loss through the jackets. May I have your views on this theory please?"

Answer: "There is no disadvantage in having light-alloy cylinders in small sizes. The jacket loss is only minutely greater than with cast iron, whereas unwanted heat is efficiently dissipated. I grant you, however, that it is true to say that the smaller the cylinder the less advantage there is from using light alloys."

Noise Eliminators

Question: "What is the purpose of the vertical webs in the cylinder finning?"

Answer: "These are purely noise eliminators. They cut down 'ring,' and it is an interesting fact that they increase the sound-wave periodicity of the fins to such an extent that a proportion of the noise emitted is beyond the range of the human ear."

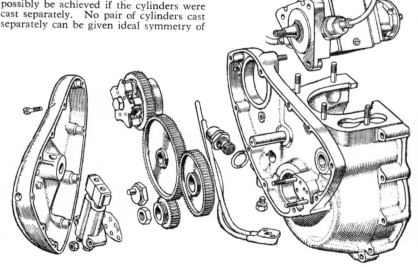

Military Triumph

a Questionnaire Dealing with the Services Hybrid

ILSON

Question: "Will you tell me why cast iron is used for the cylinder liner? And will you please explain also how it is inserted into the 'muff'? What are its special properties that make it suitable as a liner material? Is there not a big difference between the rate of expansion of cast iron and that of the light alloy used for the block?"

Answer: "A high-grade, close-grained cast iron is a most effective cylinder liner material on the score of its good wearing qualities; because of its natural graphite content it is somewhat self-lubricating; it has the property of 'oil wetness'—if there is such an expression. To take an opposite example, highly polished chromium will not remain wet when oil is splashed on it. This characteristic does not apply to chromium alone; it is a curious phenomenon which exists in many metals with widely differing structures. With regard to the final part of your question, the liners are pressed into the light-alloy cylinder

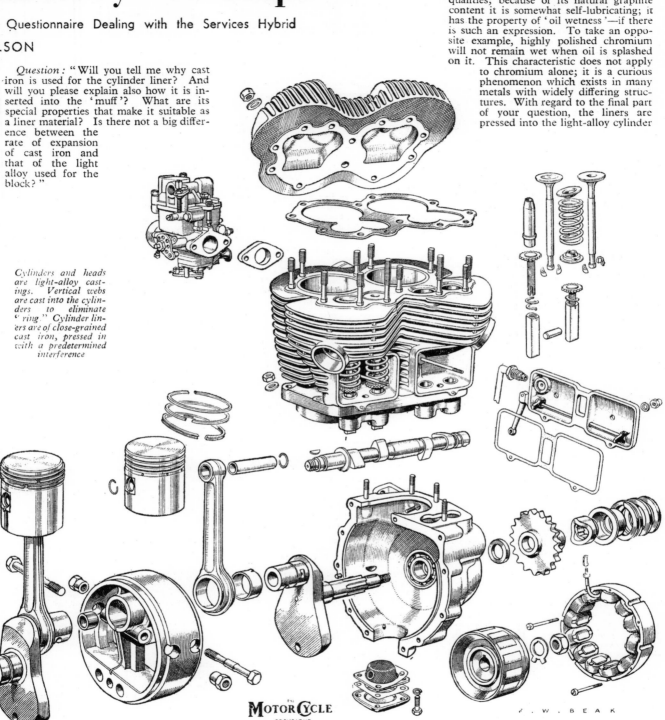

Cylinders and heads are light-alloy castings. Vertical webs are cast into the cylinders to eliminate 'ring.' Cylinder liners are of close-grained cast iron, pressed in with a predetermined interference

MOTOR CYCLE
COPYRIGHT

F. W. BEAK

Unusual features of the engine are the pinch-bolt-type built up crankshaft; light-alloy, one-piece connecting rods; and the single camshaft mounted across the front of the crankcase. Tappet heads have serrated edges for adjustment by means of a special spanner which pivots about the cylinder holding-down studs

Modern Engines: Military Triumph

bores with a predetermined interference fit. I grant that there are big differences between the rates of expansion of cast iron and light alloy. But with the use of a low-expansion alloy, the difference is greatly reduced and, indeed, rendered ineffective, as a result of the heat having to travel first through the cast iron before reaching the alloy jacket. Thus the cast iron continues to expand and increase its contact with the light-alloy 'muff' until the alloy cools it to the point where equilibrium is reached. Although there are advocates of bonding the aluminium jacket to the iron liner, bonding is unnecessary in this case. Our own application of bimetal construction, as exemplified in both the TR5 and the T100 engines, works perfectly."

Question: "Is there any special point of note concerning the pistons?"

Answer: "No, they are Lo-Ex pistons and straightforward in every way."

Question: "The valve seats are of cast iron and cast in. Why are they cast in, when the cylinder liners are pressed in?"

Answer: "The material used is actually a particularly high-grade cast iron, one that has proved to be most satisfactory. The seats, you will note, are cast integrally with one another. This is done to provide sufficient metal round the seats and maintain close centres. Were the seats cast separately, with an equal amount of metal round them, the centres would have to be spread—and this could only be done to the detriment of the combustion-chamber shape. Casting them in provides a sound area of contact and eliminates a good deal of machining. The cylinder liners, on the other hand, do not require to be cast in, since they are perfectly symmetrical tubes which can easily and practically be pressed in. By virtue of their being pressed in, the liners are, of course, replaceable."

Inclined Valves

Question: "What is the purpose of having the valves inclined in a fore-and-aft direction at two degrees to the vertical?"

Answer: "Inclining the valves allows us to have greater section of metal between the exhaust ports and the cylinder bores. Another reason is that the valve springs are farther away from the hotter portions of the cylinder and thus retain their efficiency over long periods. I would use an even greater angle if this were geometrically possible without spreading the timing gears too far. An incidental advantage accruing from having the valves inclined is that some improvement results in the combustion chamber and exhaust port shapes."

Question: "Will you explain, please, why phosphor bronze is used for the valve guides?"

Answer: "It must be borne in mind that this light-alloy twin is not a cheap engine. It is built with the best materials throughout. And phosphor bronze is the ideal material for valve guides in light-alloy cylinders. So far as the exhaust valve is concerned, the phosphor bronze guide, with its high conductivity, has the advantage of extracting the maximum heat from the valve. A beautiful bearing surface develops in the inlet guide bore. Although cast iron could be used, phosphor bronze is infinitely more suitable. Indeed, when it was intended to offer this engine to the public with a cast-iron cylinder block, it was the intention to retain the phosphor bronze valve guides. By the way, the reasons for the cast-iron engine job not going into production were chiefly concerned with material shortages."

Question: "What is the reason for the serrated-type tappet heads?"

Answer: "It is a question of ease of adjustment. There are no lock nuts, as you can see. A special tool with serrations corresponding with those in the tappet head is provided in the tool kit. A projecting lug at the head of the tool is drilled so that it can be located on an appropriate cylinder-base stud. This done, and the tool's serrations meshed with those of the tappet, the tool is pivoted about the stud, thus screwing or unscrewing the tappet head as required. The tappet head is locked by means of a light spring, the upper tail of which engages with a 'click' action in small indentations on the underside of the head."

Induction Pipe

Question: "I note that the induction pipe appears to undergo a change in cross-section where it passes between the cylinder bores. Why is this so?"

Answer: "The induction pipe does not actually change its cross-sectional area. It merely changes its shape. We could employ an induction pipe of constant shape if the bores were spread wider. But there would be the disadvantage of less rigidity—because of the longer crankshaft—and wider cylinder centres would mean a larger block and thus increased weight."

Question: "On the face of things, this particular induction pipe has a very compact form and the warming of the mixture where it passes between the bores should help atomization. But is it not so that a cooling mixture passing between the bores at this particular point will encourage distortion in cooling the area round it? And that volumetric efficiency and combustion efficiency will be lower as a result of the charge being pre-heated?"

Answer: "Part of the scheme of passing the mixture between the bores is actually to provide reasonable cooling at a critical point in the engine and also to warm the mixture sufficiently, as you suggest, to help atomization. In practice, it is found that the mixture passes through too quickly for it to become so warm as seriously to affect volumetric efficiency. In this engine, volumetric efficiency is in any case controlled by the valve size. The amount of cooling provided by the gas in the port is not sufficient for it to cause distortion—bearing in mind the high conductivity of the surrounding sections which equalizes any great heat differential."

Question: "Why is the cylinder head a sand casting? Could it not be manufactured more easily, more quickly, more cheaply and more accurately if it were die-cast?"

Answer: "Production of the cylinder heads would be simplified by die-casting. But the quantities at the moment do not justify the high cost of dies. Should larger quantities be required, dies will be sunk for the purpose."

Hottest Area

Question: "Will you explain why, in the combustion chambers, the sparking-plug bosses are offset towards the exhaust ports?"

Answer: "Combustion-chamber shape and the location of the sparking plug have an important bearing on the tendency or otherwise of a side-valve engine to pink. It is an advantage to fire the compressed mixture from the hottest zone of the head. In this engine the hottest area is that above the exhaust-valve head.

Question: "A pinch-bolt type of built-up crankshaft is employed. Its design is quite different from that used in the present production range. What are the advantages in this particular application?"

Answer: "The underlying aim behind this crankshaft (which was used so successfully in the 3T Triumph) is to provide for one-piece big-ends. Mechanical limitations permitting, the one-piece big-end is always preferable to one of the split type. One reason is that the split big-end suffers from vulnerability of the big-end bolts—which are the most highly stressed metal components in the engine. Another argument against the use of split big-ends in this engine is that the skill required to fit them properly may not always be available in, say, a field unit. The one-piece connecting rod is less costly to produce than its split counterpart. The pinch-bolt design of crankshaft does, incidentally, have

---

TECHNICAL DATA

CAPACITY : 499 c.c.

BORE : 63 mm.

STROKE : 80 mm.

COMPRESSION RATIO : 6 to 1.

PISTON RING END-GAP : 0.010-0.014in ; side clearance (compression rings), 0.001-0.003in ; scraper, 0.0025-0.005in.

PISTON CLEARANCES : top land, 0.012-0.015in ; second land, 0.010-0.012in ; top of skirt, 0.0065-0.006in ; bottom of skirt, 0.0045-0.004in.

VALVE SPRING FREE LENGTH : 1$\frac{11}{16}$in.

TAPPET CLEARANCE : inlet, 0.002in ; exhaust, 0.004in ; when cold.

VALVE TIMING : (with no tappet clearance) inlet valve begins to open 16 degrees before top dead centre and closes 56 degrees after bottom dead centre ; exhaust valve begins to open 56 degrees before bottom dead centre and closes 16 degrees after top dead centre.

IGNITION TIMING : On full advance, contact-breaker points just beginning to separate 21 degrees of crankshaft rotation or when the piston is $\frac{1}{8}$in before top dead centre.

ENGINE DIMENSIONS : drive-side crankshaft ball bearing, 1$\frac{3}{8}$in bore, 2$\frac{13}{16}$in outside diameter, 1$\frac{3}{16}$in wide ; plain bearing, timing-side shaft, diameter 1$\frac{3}{8}$ x 1$\frac{1}{8}$in long ; crankpin diameter, 1.5in ; gudgeon pin diameter, $\frac{5}{8}$in ; big-end to small-end centres, 6.5in ; inlet and exhaust valve head diameter, 1$\frac{13}{16}$in ; seat angle, 45 degrees ; valve lift, 0.3in.

CARBURETTOR : Solex type 26 WH-2 ; No. 22 choke ; 110 main jet.

---

its limitations at ultra-high speeds, when the journals are likely to bend under high-inertia loadings, but it is perfectly satisfactory in this particular application.

Question: "How is true alignment of the crankpins and main-bearing journals ensured during manufacture?"

Answer: "This is obtained primarily by first-class machining of the crankshaft halves and flywheel. There are alignment holes in the flywheel and crankshaft through which a ground rod is passed during assembly. The rod is a push fit—neither slack nor tight—and the system provides truth commensurate with commercial requirements."

Question: "I note that 3 per cent nickel steel is used for the half crankshafts. What are the reasons behind its use?"

Answer: "In order to keep the overall length of the crankshaft down as much as possible, the shaft throws are very slender. They must therefore be made of strong material. Alloy steel containing nickel is stronger than plain carbon steels or even manganese steels, and it has a higher elastic limit; therefore it is less prone to fatigue."

Bending Moment

Question: "The axial length of the crankshaft between the centres of the main bearings is 6½ inches. Is there a greater bending moment with this crankshaft than there is with, say, the Speed Twin crankshaft, or is it less?"

Answer: "Actually, there is very little bending moment with either crankshaft. If one shaft is superior to the other, then the TRW shaft scores because the distance between the supporting bearing centres is shorter."

Question: "The forward part of the inner half of the primary-chain case is cast integrally with the crankcase. What is the reason for this?"

Answer: "The reason is that part of the primary case houses the stator for the A.C. generator. Casting the primary case register integral with the crankcase ensures concentricity of the stator and the rotor, which is, of course, mounted on the drive-side mainshaft."

Question: "Spur-gear drive to the

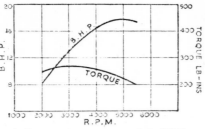

Torque and power curves of the TRW Triumph

magneto and camshaft is employed. Would not a single, triangular chain drive have been simpler from a production point of view?"

Answer: "On cost, gears are the cheaper, because the purchase price of a chain in itself is greatly in excess of the cost of gears cut in our own factory. Moreover, no chain drive is as reliable as gears, and with the latter, no tension-adjustment problems arise. A triangular chain drive was employed on an experimental side-valve twin made by this company during the war, but it suffered from the disadvantage that it was not possible to have enough teeth on the driving sprocket to achieve a really good arc of contact. One always endeavours to keep the aluminium bulk of a timing-case to the minimum, and it is possible to keep the case smaller when gears are used."

Camshaft Bearings

Question: "The EN32 case-hardening steel single camshaft is carried in phosphor bronze bushes. Did you consider the use of roller bearings for this work? I would have thought that the camshaft bearings would be subject to fairly severe bending loads."

Answer: Any form of roller or ball bearing is ruled out for this application on the score of expense. Camshaft bearings are, as you suggest, subject to severe whip loads, particularly at certain r.p.m. But these are catered for in the elementary stages of design. The shaft is made of such section as to keep the whip within reasonable limits. Actually, these camshaft bushes have a reasonably easy life

and they should outlast the rest of the engine. Their running clearance more than caters for temporary malalignment caused by such whip as takes place."

Question: "Would not whip be eliminated completely if the shaft were supported in the middle by means of a third bearing?"

Answer: "Not necessarily; one does not use bearings except when they are necessary. As you see, the section of the camshaft is increased in the middle. Were a bearing fitted there, the ring would have to be large and the rubbing speeds would be fairly high. Moreover, assembly would be complicated and would require the bearing to be split. However, if the engine were an o.h.v. designed for high r.p.m. and high power output, I agree that a middle bearing would be necessary. But in this engine, with moderate valve-spring pressure there is just no need for one."

A.C. Generator

Question: "Why is it that this engine employs a magneto for ignition and a B.T.-H. A.C. generator for lighting purposes? Would not the generator provide enough current to energize an ignition coil as well as feed the bulbs and horn?"

Answer: "A magneto is employed because at the time this specification was compiled, the A.C. generator unit was not developed sufficiently. In my view no motor cycle should depend on its battery for starting purposes. This problem, however, has now been overcome in more modern developments; if this engine had been designed today I would scrap the magneto and employ an A.C. generator in conjunction with battery and coil ignition."

Question: "I note that the engine breather is taken from the valve chest. What is the reason for this?"

Answer: "One should always endeavour to allow the engine to breathe from the highest point, since the gases which one aims to release rise rather than drop."

Question: "And what is the power output?"

Answer: "Here are power and torque curves—you may publish them if you wish."

Gas Turbine

Can the Turbine Rival the Piston Engine?

THE late Henry Ford once said that there might, at any moment, be some lone individual working in some small back room who may bring out something that would completely revolutionize the world of motoring or commerce (I cannot remember his exact words but they were to that effect). The Whittle jet is doing this to the world of aviation at this very moment, but the odds on it ousting the piston engine in motor cycles and cars are very much against it without some drastic rearrangement.

The greatest efficiency from the fuel consumption point of view is dependent upon reaching the highest possible temperature that can be attained when the ignited gas is doing its work. It is amazing that in the cylinder of an internal-combustion engine the temperature of the explosion reaches a figure well over 3,000 degrees Centigrade, while the melting point of the cylinder is only 1,200 deg C., and that of the piston only about 700 deg C.

In a gas turbine, a comparatively low gas temperature must be used as the gas has to "play" upon thin blades in the manner of a blow-lamp, and piston engine combustion temperatures are comparable with those of an oxy-acetylene flame; which the blades will certainly not stand up to. Thus the gas turbine's efficiency on the ground is less than one-half that of the piston engine. It is true that in the latter we lose 25 per cent into the cooling fins and about 38 per cent out of the exhaust.

If the gas turbine could beat the internal-combustion engine in these two spheres, it might have a chance to catch up, but as at present designed it cannot; though, with the concentration of grey matter now engaged upon gas turbine work, one never knows what brilliant new scheme may enter the arena. The turbine experts have been talking about improving the fuel economy for more than three years, but they appear to be now agreed that, with present types, the most that can be expected is a further 5 per cent.

One would have thought that the real sphere for present types of gas turbines is in the ousting of the steam engines, because with steam we have the appalling loss of heat up the chimney, the big loss in converting water into steam, and the exhaust waste. These losses are so great that in a good steam loco on the railway we get only 4 b.h.p. at the wheels for the equivalent of 100 h.p. fed as coal into the furnace.—"TECHNICUS."

Road and Race

VIC WILLOUGHBY Selects a Machine, Sees it B

Alignment of the crankshaft assembly is checked on vee-blocks by means of dial gauges calibrated to 0·0005in

THE present is a time of specialization. If a motor cyclist wishes to indulge a serious fancy for racing, he may think in terms of a new machine costing upward of £400. For such a price he can buy a highly specialized piece of megaphoned machinery whose engine performance, road holding, braking and navigational qualities will be ideally suited to his racing purposes. But this machine will be useless for other forms of motor cycling. Should his taste be for the less spectacular sphere of touring or his needs be purely utilitarian, the present-day market offers him, at a considerably lower price level, a selection of mounts appropriate to these more modest requirements. Likewise, machines in the latter category are of no practical use for racing purposes.

What if a man's aspirations embrace both racing and roadster work? Two separate machines can easily cost him a total of £600-£650—a sum far beyond the scope of the majority of motor cyclists.

Twenty odd years ago, the problem was easier of solution. Specialization, particularly among over - the - counter machines, had not approached its present level and many riders did, in fact, use one machine quite successfully for the two divergent purposes. A super-sports machine of that era was tractable enough for public-road use. Shorn of its lights at the weekend and fitted with a higher-compression piston, smaller engine or gear box sprocket, knobbly tyres and, possibly, high-lift cams, it provided its owner with a performance which enabled him to enjoy an afternoon's grass-track racing or what-have-you without disgracing himself. Frequently it would be in harness again the following day as a ride-to-work mount.

Today, with the increasing popularity of Clubman's events at race meetings, there is a demand for reasonably priced dual-purpose machines which will permit a revival of the erstwhile clubman-cum-racer. A few such models are already available. In an endeavour to assess the suitability of one of their number for the dual role, I investigated the claims of the 498 c.c. Triumph Tiger 100c.

Introduced for 1953 and retailing for little over £220, the T100c succeeds last year's T100 with separate conversion kit. Since the new model is fitted as standard with racing camshafts, the owner is relieved of the difficulty

Crankshaft balancing. Len Docker prepares to drill a hole in a flywheel periphery while Vic Willoughby inspects a crankshaft assembly on the Stellited knife-edges

Convertible Twin

Rides it in Town and Country and Races it at Snetterton

of changing camshafts—a job which entails parting the crankcase halves. Other items of racing significance which are standard fitments are twin carburettors and a large-capacity oil tank. The machine is normally supplied in road-going trim (i.e., with silencers, electrical equipment, etc.) and is readily adaptable to racing trim by a standard routine of removals and substitutions. Items for removal include the electrical equipment, stands, number plates and kick-starter (if permitted by the race regulations). Substitutions concern the exhaust system, handlebar, footrests (a folding right-hand racing rest can be supplied if required to permit use of the kick-starter), carburettor jets, sparking plugs and rev indicator (in place of speedometer). To suit the rearward footrests, the brake pedal is moved back and a shorter brake rod fitted, and the gear pedal is turned through 180 degrees on its splined shaft. If required, higher-compression pistons and close-ratio gears are available.

Standard Production Methods

It is apparent, in view of the competitive price of the T100c, that no abnormal production methods could be considered in its assembly. This fact was amply proved to me when I saw a batch of these models being built. Standard production processes are used throughout, as normal Triumph tolerances are considered quite suitable for machines intended for Clubman racing. As far as the operators are concerned, it is immaterial whether their components are destined for use in a 5T or a T100c. For my test machine, I picked an engine at random from the assembly line.

I watched every process in the building of the engine and its assembly into the machine, and was impressed by the combination of speed and a consistently high standard of accuracy and cleanliness. Time-saving devices abound (time is an expensive commodity) and compressed-air lines are liberally employed. Let me take you on a conducted tour to witness the building of a T100c.

We will start in the engine assembly bay—the responsibility of genial Frank Baker, whose pre-war experience included working with Noel Pope at Brooklands. Here we

Frank Baker (chief of the engine assembly dept.) and the author watch the T100c engine undergoing bench test

see the crankshafts bolted to the central flywheel by means of six ¼in, 60-ton, ground-steel bolts. Two of the bolt holes in each component are reamered to exact size to ensure accurate alignment of the assembly. The assembly is then fitted with two "slave" main bearings, lowered on to vee-blocks and checked for alignment. No more than half-a-thou eccentricity is permitted on the shafts, but machining accuracy is such that remedial treatment is rarely required. Split balance weights, equal to the rotating masses and 65 per cent of the reciprocating masses, are fitted to the big-end journals and the assembly is then placed on Stellited knife-edges to check static balance. The flywheel rim is drilled radially to achieve the desired result. Complete connecting rods are weighed, paired and bolted to the big-end journals; no fitting is required.

Matched Timing Gears

At the next bench we see a girl working on a drive-side half crankcase. She fits the mainshaft ball race and the sintered-bronze camshaft bushes with the aid of a hand press, taps home the two crankcase-locating dowels and the breather disc, and screws in various studs with a power tool. Meanwhile, the timing-side case is similarly treated; an operator presses in the camshaft bushes, chip shield (which keeps foreign matter from the bearings), mainshaft roller bearing and intermediate timing gear spindle and verifies the freedom of the oilways with a compressed-air line. This crankcase half is passed to the next bench, where its internal oil scavenge pipe is fitted before the casting is placed on a jig for matching of the timing gears. The two camshafts are then threaded through their bushes and their gears keyed in position, using, first, the marked keyway. In each gear three keyways are provided which allow valve timing variations of five degrees.

The crankcase halves have previously been machined in pairs and marked accordingly. The next operator, introduced as Joe, bolts the appropriate halves together over the crankshaft assembly, using a trace of jointing compound between the mating faces. That done, he checks each camshaft for freedom of rotation, bolts the oil filter to the base of the case and places the complete unit on a sliding jig on the assembly track. Joe's neighbour fits over the appropriate cylinder-base studs the two dowels which ensure accurate cylinder-block alignment. Having tapped the half-time pinion on to the timing-side mainshaft, he then completes the timing-gear train by meshing the intermediate pinion to the marks provided.

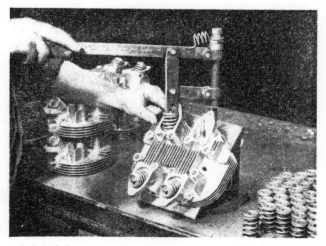

Deft Irish fingers insert the split cotters during assembly of the valves and valve springs

Stan Truslove (assistant i c engine test bay) checks the magneto timing with a degree plate and a 0·0015in feeler gauge. Note the dial indicator on a valve-spring cap for the valve-timing check

Half-a-pint of engine oil is poured into the crankcase. The gudgeon pins are slipped into the connecting rods and carefully checked for squareness with the crankcase mouth. This check proving satisfactory, pistons and rings are fitted to the rods and painted with graphited oil. Ring clamps are placed in position and the cylinder block is lowered over the pistons faster than I am able to jot down brief notes of the operations. Standard pistons give a compression ratio of 8 to 1. I decided to be awkward and specify 9 to 1 pistons, since the regulations for the race meeting where I proposed to test the T100c permitted the use of petrol-benzole fuel.

Bench Test

The cylinder base nuts are fitted and rapidly tightened before the unit is slid along to the next man, who fits the front engine plates, dynamo, magneto and oil pump. Purely for reasons of personal time-saving at a later date, I requested omission of the dynamo from my chosen engine. We pass along to Ted, who times the ignition to $\frac{3}{8}$in before t.d.c. provided standard pistons are fitted. If high-compression pistons have been specified, the timing process is done later in the engine-test bay, using a degree plate and working to a figure of 43 degrees before t.d.c.

The previously assembled cylinder head is now fitted; its bolts are run down with a power-driven spanner and finally tightened by hand. As push-rods, tubes and rocker boxes rapidly take their places, the engine assumes a more normal appearance. Finally, the last operator on the assembly track fits the oil-drain Y-pipes, screws in the exhaust-pipe stubs and adjusts the valve clearances.

Before following the completed engine across to the engine-test bay, we can see some of the sub-assemblies being prepared. The cylinder-head assembly is a good example. The bare casting is received from the machine shop and, first, its four cast-iron valve guides are fitted under a press. The head is then placed on a jig on a vertical drilling

machine and its valve seats cut and "topped" by cutters which pilot in the valve guides. Valve grinding is an education. The valves are oscillated rapidly in pairs by air-operated lappers, and the desired result is achieved in as many seconds as minutes are normally required when the job is done by hand.

Valve timing is checked with the aid of a degree plate in the engine-test bay. Readings are taken when the valves are 0.020in off their seats. Correct figures are then 34 degrees either side of t.d.c., and 55 degrees either side of b.d.c. My engine proved to be within two degrees of these figures, so that use of the alternative camwheel keyways was not required.

The engine was put on the dynamometer for test. After being motored round for a while and then warmed up under power, it was given full throttle at 6,000 and 7,000 r.p.m.—with silencers, of course. At these speeds it pulled 26lb, which represented approximately 35 and 40 b.h.p. respectively.

Rapid Progress

I followed my engine over to the machine assembly line, whose chief is Sid Tubb—a man who recalls Isle of Man T.T. races of the pre-first world war era. Here I found frame, fork, wheels, mudguards, handlebar and oil tank already assembled and a girl waiting to pounce with wiring harness and c.v.c. unit. These latter items I declined—again for purely personal time-saving. The machine was wheeled on to a ramp for fitting of gear box and rear chain, and then moved on to the finishing track. Here it progressed rapidly with operators working on both sides of the track. Engine, chaincase, primary drive—all were fitted and adjusted and soon a gleaming T100c was wheeled off the end of the track.

Normally, the head lamp is fitted at this stage, and oil tank, gear box and chaincase are filled before the machine is motored round on rollers via its rear tyre for half an hour at a speed equivalent to 35 m.p.h. in top gear. A 10-15 miles' road test follows before final adjustment and cleaning. I took my machine from the end of the track, however, for a quick check of riding position, etc., prior to a trip to the M.I.R.A. proving ground. As my head-lamp nacelle contained no lighting switch, I decided to re-run the front-brake cable through the vacant hole to provide a better sweep. Lighter control was achieved, but on full fork extension the cable proved to be too short in its new position, and a new cable was made up some 2in longer.

On arrival at M.I.R.A., the racing exhaust pipes, No. 180 main jets and racing sparking plugs were fitted. Still clad in storm coat and waders, I took the Triumph through the

A routine of removals and substitutions converts the T100c from roadster to racing mount

timed section in both directions, registering almost 100 m.p.h. Some clutch slip set in after a few runs, however, and although standing starts with a megaphoned engine and an 8.5 to 1 bottom gear (I had specified the close ratios for racing purposes) are not the kindest of treatment for a standard cork clutch, the impression was gained that a little extra pressure on the clutch springs during assembly might have obviated the bother. For safety, I returned to the works and had the clutch fitted with heavier springs and shorter cups.

Eventually, I left for London. The Tiger resembled a laden Christmas tree with its racing exhaust pipes, megaphones and spare footrests strapped on. It would, of course, be ludicrous to expect a dual-purpose machine to fill either the touring or the racing role as well as would a specialist machine. It was soon apparent that the man who buys a Tiger 100c, with its racing camshafts, *purely* for public-road use is acting unwisely. These cams are not designed for use with silencers; in consequence, the machine's road performance was neither so flexible nor so potent as that of a standard Tiger 100. At 4,000 r.p.m., the speed at which this engine " comes on the megaphone," the conflict between cams and silencers was most pronounced, there being a noticeable reduction in torque at that engine speed.

Minor Modifications

On the open road, I cruised at speeds up to 5,200 r.p.m. in top gear (approximately 80 m.p.h.). Further throttle opening at that speed, however, resulted in a certain amount of pinking—the compression ratio, as mentioned earlier, was 9 to 1. In town, the high bottom gear and compression ratio demanded intelligent use of throttle, clutch and ignition controls when getting away from a standstill. Nevertheless, an experienced motor cyclist, after a modicum of practice, would experience little difficulty in riding such a machine happily on the public road, except in heavy traffic; even then, 8 to 1 pistons and the standard 12.2 to 1 bottom gear ratio would doubtless provide the desired degree of tractability.

Arrived home, I carried out a few minor modifications to suit my personal preferences and to render the machine more suitable for racing. The handlebar orifices in the nacelle were filed out to enable the racing bar to be swivelled to a suitable angle. A chain link was fitted to the front brake lever to reduce the hand reach required for its operation. In an effort to lighten the twistgrip action, the twin throttle cables were rerun outside the nacelle and each throttle spring was cut ¼in shorter. The clutch cable was also rerun—at both ends—with beneficial results since the heavier clutch springs were in use. Finally, the front wheel was balanced.

Tiger at Snetterton

The Tiger was then ridden to the home of a colleague nearer to the Snetterton circuit and the standard conversion routine carried out. After a brief gallop with the model in racing trim, the footrests and brake pedal were cut and welded, and a rectangular piece of sponge rubber was attached to the tank-top grid for chin protection.

The final part of my test of the T100c took place on Saturday, May 2, at the Snetterton airfield race meeting. It was four years since I had competed at an airfield additionally, the opposition was considerably stronger than that which would normally confront a clubman's racing machine. Nevertheless, the Triumph put up an excellent show and was not approached by any other standard clubman-racer. Throughout the meeting, it was headed only by expertly ridden 499 c.c. featherbed Manx Nortons, Maurice Cann's 496 c.c. Gambalunga Moto-Guzzi and the twin-cylinder Pike-B.S.A.

The standard Triumph put up a splendid show among pukka racing machines

The practice session showed that the standard 22-tooth engine sprocket was too large for this circuit, and a change to a 21-tooth sprocket enabled the engine to achieve 7,000 r.p.m. in top gear. At this engine speed, a high-frequency vibration proved troublesome. It resulted in the splitting of a weld at the base of the fuel tank, and made it difficult for me to keep the throttle wide open for the length of the Norwich straight, in spite of my previous shortening of the return springs. Two weaker-than-standard throttle springs which had been submitted for test by a reader were an improvement. On the curves I found that the prop-stand grounded on the left, while the right-hand megaphone clip was soon wiped off! The prop-stand was removed and a new clip was fitted with its bolt above the exhaust pipe.

I was, at first, apprehensive concerning the clutch, but my fears proved to be groundless; at no point on the circuit was it necessary to come off the megaphone and slip the clutch. Furthermore, I found its task could be eased by making all upward gear changes quite cleanly without the clutch, such was the closeness of the gear ratios. However, I was loath to slip the clutch much at the start of each race and, though the engine fired readily, several places were lost waiting for the engine speed to build up to 4,000 r.p.m. with the clutch home.

Afternoon's Great Fun

As implied earlier, a dual-purpose machine must inevitably fall short of the performance of a specialist machine in any particular sphere. In the matter of engine power, I was delighted to find that the Triumph enabled me to scrap with the riders of pukka racing machines of nearly twice its cost. Its steering and braking at very high speeds, however, were not quite up to the same high standard. In the 500 c.c. heat, the Tiger finished close behind Maurice Cann's Moto-Guzzi which, in turn, was astern the Nortons of J. Surtees, M. O'Rourke and P. Harrison. In the final, an unfavourable starting-grid position proved a handicap and, though Surtees won the race from an even worse start, I was, of course, not able to match the speed of his famous Norton, the power of his large Italian front brake or his personal prowess. Nevertheless, only similar Nortons and the Pike-B.S.A. finished in front of the Tiger.

The 1,000 c.c. heat brought me third place behind the " featherbeds " of O'Rourke and R. H. King, while in the final of the same event I was able to scrap closely for the whole race with Denis Parkinson's well-known Norton, and eventually finished fifth.

Certainly, the T100c had given me an afternoon's great fun. Its performance as a clubman-racer in such distinguished company proved that it could amply fill the sporting, in addition to the touring, role. In the less severe competition of clubman's races it is a potential winner, with the inestimable advantage that it can be ridden to and from the course.

ROAD TESTS of CURRENT MODELS—

Clean lines and pleasant styling are prominent features of the "Speed Twin."

The 498 c.c. Model 5T
TRIUMPH
"SPEED TWIN"

Latest Version of a Popular o.h.v. "Multi" with Unorthodox Electrical Equipment

ALTHOUGH it is not strictly true to say that the "Speed Twin" Triumph was the first machine to be powered by the side-by-side vertical twin-cylinder engine which now enjoys widespread popularity, few would deny that it led the way towards the vertical-twin trend. Again, this machine is not the first on which both lighting and ignition requirements are taken care of, basically, by a stator/rotor A.C. generator, but it seems likely, however, that the "Speed Twin" will once again give a lead likely to be followed by others in due course, for the model under review, fitted with a Lucas RM12 A.C. generator, proved conclusively that this system of " electrics " has everything to commend it.

Widely condemned in the past for a variety of reasons, notably, the dependence upon dynamo and battery, coil-ignition systems have usually been confined to small machines of medium performance and fitted largely as an economy expedient. With modern A.C./D.C. coil-ignition equipment, however, the bogy of a flat battery and, therefore, difficult starting, is overcome.

Moreover, whilst critics have sought from time to time to prove that the coil-ignition system, though suitable for medium-performance models, is at a disadvantage at high engine speeds, a glance at the accompanying test report indicates that this opinion is unfounded.

Add to these advantages the compactness factor and the reduction in the number of auxiliary drives, and it becomes obvious that the stator/rotor generator with an A.C./D.C. rectifier, as fitted to the "Speed Twin," has come to stay.

Establishing a good reputation from the start, the ignition system provided a fat spark at all times. From cold, the lever controlling the air slide, mounted beneath the saddle, was used, but could, almost

---

TESTER'S ROAD REPORT

Maximum Speeds in :—

                                         Time from Standing Start

Top Gear (Ratio 5·0 to 1) __91__ m.p.h. = 5850 r.p.m. __41__ secs.

Third Gear (Ratio 5·95 to 1) __84__ m.p.h. = 6350 r.p.m. __25__ secs.

Second Gear (Ratio 8·45 to 1) __64__ m.p.h. = 6700 r.p.m. __13¾__ secs.

Speeds over measured Quarter Mile :—

Flying Start __86__ m.p.h.   Standing Start __52·94__ m.p.h.

Braking Figures On DRY TARMAC Surface, from 30 m.p.h. :—

Both Brakes __32__ ft.   Front Brake __39__ ft   Rear Brake __51__ ft.

Fuel Consumption :—

30 m.p.h. __96__ m.p.g.   ~~40 m.p.h.~~ ~~m.p.g.~~   50 m.p.h. __62__ m.p.g.

Acceleration graph — M.P.H. vs. SECONDS, showing:
SPEED AT END OF STANDING ¼ MILE → MAX. IN TOP, MAX. IN THIRD, MAX. IN SECOND, CHANGE points for BOTTOM, SECOND, THIRD, TOP gears.

" Maintenance . with reasonable facility." (Above) Adjusting the contact breaker, and (below) the clutch.

A comfortable riding position adds to the pleasures of high speed touring on the "5T."

immediately, be fully opened when the engine had started. When thoroughly warm, the unit settled down to an even tickover, guaranteed to continue without stalling. Carburation was well suited to the engine characteristics and the machine responded without hesitation when the twistgrip was turned from the shut to a fully open position.

Another feature of the model is the rubber shock absorber incorporated in the clutch centre. This consists of a series of rubber blocks, located between vanes on the clutch hub, which absorb transmission shocks.

No difficulty was experienced in arranging a comfortable riding position. Footrests, rear brake and gearchange pedals are all provided with a range of adjustment, and the usual Triumph-pattern handlebars can be raised or lowered as necessary. Hand controls are clipped to the bars and can be set to conform to individual requirements. A neat horn button, screwed into the handlebar near the left grip, is inconspicuous, for the wire is taken inside the handlebar tube. It is, together with the dipswitch on the right-hand side, conveniently placed and easy to operate.

That comment applied also to the remainder of the controls, either hand or foot, and the clutch in particular was noted for its light, smooth operation. Perhaps a reduction in the effort needed to operate the front brake would be a useful detail improvement.

Provided that the clutch was freed before the engine was started, first gear could be engaged noiselessly. No difficulty was experienced in selecting neutral. From first to second and from second to third gears, a slight pause was necessary to ensure satisfying changes, but no thought or hesitation was necessary when changing up to, or down from, top gear. Gear changes were quite positive at any speed, and could, if desired, be made as fast as physically possible.

Acceleration was more than adequate and the machine could quickly be whipped up to a cruising gait of 70 m.p.h. This maintained speed proved to be well within the machine's capabilities and left a useful reserve of power should the need to use it arise. Throughout the normally-used engine range there appeared to be no vibration period; there was slight vibration at wide throttle openings only, but it was very minor.

Although possessing high performance, the machine was particularly tractable and pleasant to ride at "about town" speeds.

It was quite happy below 30 m.p.h. in top gear. Transmission snatch was never experienced.

Within the limits of the available movement, the spring-wheel absorbed road shock and was at its best on fast main roads. At high speeds, on second- or third-rate surfaces, a little pitching was experienced, but this, although requiring that the footrests be used to take some of the rider's weight, did not affect the handling or steering. Really bad roads could be traversed at fairly high speeds, for the front wheel, controlled by the hydraulically damped front forks, remained "on line" at all times.

On wet or dry roads, the two brakes worked admirably. An earlier note concerning the effort needed to operate the front brake implies no criticism of its function as a "stopper." In spite of a considerable mileage in the Welsh mountains, no brake-fade was experienced, no uncertainty arose, and no adjustment was necessary. The large-diameter rear brake required only light pressures, and the arrangement of the linkage gave smooth, progressive retardation.

Generally, the machine is adequately silent. Engine noise has been held to a low level and the transmission is inaudible when working. Without employing excessive care with throttle openings, the exhaust note was subdued at speeds below the legal town limit and rose to a pleasant burble when cruising.

Varying road conditions make reference to night cruising difficult. Generally, however, the main beam of the sealed unit in the nacelle provided enough light for a maintained speed in excess of 60 m.p.h. on good main roads. In the dipped position, the beam caused no apparent annoyance. A recent amendment to the lighting equipment is the current use of a combined "stop" and "tail" lamp, control for the stop lamp being exercised by a switch operated when the footbrake is used. Voltage-drop in the rectification process was negligible and the generator kept the battery well up to scratch.

Mudguarding is neatly done and efficient in use, although the inevitable spray from the contact point between tyre and road has not been completely checked. A prop-stand on the near side of the machine, now has a useful extension ensuring easy operation.

A high standard of cleanliness was noted at the termination of the test and both engine and gearbox were oiltight.

Normal maintenance tasks can be carried out with reasonable facility, although some owners may not possess the manual dexterity of the "works" personnel necessary when replacing the lower distributor clip.

Generally, the latest "Speed Twin" has been enhanced in appearance by the change from dynamo to generator and, in traditional amaranth red, would be a proud possession for any motorcyclist.

BRIEF SPECIFICATION

Engine: Vertical twin o.h.v.; gear-driven camshafts; 63-mm. bore by 80-mm. stroke = 498 c.c.; cast-iron cylinder head and barrel; compression ratio 7 to 1; valve gear fully enclosed and positively lubricated; RR56 "H"-section hiduminium connecting rods; plain big-end bearings; crankshaft mounted on heavy-duty ball and roller bearings with central flywheel; dry-sump lubrication with dual plunger pump; timing cover fitted with oil-pressure indicator; Amal carburetter; Lucas A.C. lighting-ignition system.

Transmission: ½-in. by .305-in. primary chain, totally enclosed in polished aluminium case; ⅝-in. by ⅜-in. final-drive chain protected on upper and lower runs and positively lubricated; clutch shaft shock

absorber with rubber inserts; separate four-speed gearbox, ratios 5.00, 5.95, 8.45 and 12.20 to 1; operated by positive-stop foot-change mechanism.

Frame: Full cradle-type frame with large-diameter tapered front down tube; front and rear stands; built-in pillion foot rests.

Front forks: Triumph telescopic, hydraulically damped; incorporating nacelle head lamp and instrument panel.

Lighting: Lucas A.C. generator with Westalite rectifier; battery lighting and ignition coil; Lucas 7-in. built-in head lamp.

Wheels: WM 2-19-in. Dunlop rims with 3.25-in. by 19-in. front tyre; 3.50-in. by 19-in. rear; 7-in. front and 8-in. rear brakes; brake lining area 32.9 sq. in.; red rims.

Tanks: All-steel welded petrol tank with quick-release filler cap, capacity 4 gallons; welded-steel oil tank, capacity 6 pints; built-in rubber knee grips.

Dimensions: Overall length, 84 in.; width, 28½ in.; wheelbase, 55 in.; saddle height, 29½ in.; ground clearance, 6 in.; weight, 378 lb.

Equipment: Smiths 120 m.p.h. chronometric, internally illuminated speedometer; adjustable saddle.

Finish: Amaranth red cellulose and chrome; cadmium-plated nuts and bolts.

Extras: Spring wheel £16 plus £3 6s. 8d. P.T. = total £19 6s. 8d.

Price: £159 plus £33 2s. 6d. P.T. = total £192 2s. 6d.

Makers: Triumph Engineering Co., Ltd., Meriden Works. Allesley, Coventry.

649 c.c. Triumph Tiger 110

Impressive O.H.V. Twin Combining Light Steering and Powerful Braking with a Performance to Delight the Sporting Rider

THE 649 c.c. Triumph Tiger 110 owes its existence largely to the demands of the American market where the primary requirement, within reasonable limits, is the highest possible power output from a given engine capacity. A tuned variant of the six-fifty Thunderbird, the T110 was introduced for 1954. Its specification included the then-new Triumph pivoted-fork rear springing and an engine incorporating a cast-iron cylinder block and cylinder head.

Most notable development for the current year is a light-alloy cylinder head of entirely new layout. The casting incorporates air passages to assist cooling; valve-seat inserts are of austenitic iron. An incidental improvement on the new head is that oil from the valve gear drains via the pushrod tubes, thus eliminating the need for external pipes. Combining a superb road potential with light handling and smooth, powerful braking, the T110 is a machine which cannot fail to impress the sporting rider. Few road burners, in truth, would ask for a higher cruising speed than the Triumph eagerly provides. Indeed, its capacity for searing acceleration and tireless, ultra-high cruising speeds is second only to the higher-performance 1,000 c.c. models of current and recent vintage.

But the Tiger 110 is not unduly obtrusive in its behaviour, for its exhaust note is reasonably well subdued no matter how hard the machine is ridden. Nor is it too intractable for use in heavy city traffic. Naturally, the high compression ratio, sporting valve timing and large port sizes necessary for such outstanding acceleration and speed from six-fifty roadsters involve some sacrifice of docility at low engine revolutions. Discreet use of the manual ignition control, however, tames the engine to a considerable degree and if, in addition, liberal use is made of the indirect gear ratios, negotiating heavy traffic need involve no irritation for the rider. Engine starting was dependable and relatively easy even in extremely cold weather, while petrol consumption was remarkably economical. In short, the T110, though primarily a high-powered sports model, is sufficiently well-mannered, manageable and economical to be employed for more modest duties without compromise.

Passing from a general survey of the model's qualities to a specific analysis of the various facets of its behaviour, it is logical to deal first with its most outstanding attribute—high open-road performance. The figures shown in the information panel speak for themselves. Yet it should be emphasized that the mean maximum speed and the quarter-mile acceleration figures would probable have been fractionally better still had less-windy conditions prevailed at the time the data were obtained. Though a very stiff wind blew only about 15 degrees off the direction of the stretch of road used, the speed loss upwind in such circumstances was not compensated by the downwind advantage.

Acceleration through the gears was scintillating and carburation clean. Even at an indicated 80 m.p.h. an exhilarating

Battery and tool kit are housed in a single, partitioned container. The tool kit is adequate for routine adjustments

Finish of the Tiger 110 is shell-blue and black enamel. With many light-alloy castings polished and the usual components chromium plated, the model is very smart

Left: Elimination of external pipes for valve-gear drainage results in a cleaner appearance of the engine. Right: Concealed between the oil tank and the battery box, the air filter did not restrict engine performance to any appreciable degree

surge forward could be produced simply by snapping the throttle wide open. To the Tiger 110, cruising at 75 m.p.h. was child's play and required only a small throttle opening. A speed of 80 m.p.h. could be held on half throttle, while a sustained 90 m.p.h. proved to be quite within the model's capabilities. The highest speedometer reading obtained with the rider sitting upright was 100 m.p.h. with a following wind.

The carrying of a pillion passenger did not substantially reduce cruising speed. With two adults (each clad in winter riding kit) occupying the dual-seat, the Triumph hummed along at a speedometer 80 m.p.h. for many consecutive miles on little more than half throttle. Opening the twistgrip fully sent the speedometer needle quickly round to the 90 m.p.h. mark. When checked for accuracy, the speedometer was found to register about 5 per cent slow at all speeds from an indicated 30 m.p.h. to the highest reading obtained—114 m.p.h. As a matter of interest the maximum-speed checks were repeated with the air filter disconnected, a bell-mouth fitted to the carburettor and the main-jet size increased from 250 to 270. No difference in speed was perceptible.

Engine vibration was detectable through the petrol tank from about 80 m.p.h. upward (or from a lower speed when the tank was full). Though pronounced, the tremor was not objectionable so long as the rider refrained from gripping the tank between his knees.

Maintenance of a steady 30 m.p.h. in built-up areas required a partially retarded ignition setting if top gear was used. Alternatively, third gear could be employed with the ignition control at full advance. Idling, once the engine had reached its normal working temperature, was slow and regular with the throttle closed and the ignition fully retarded or nearly so. With these conditions fulfilled, bottom gear could be engaged almost noiselessly; but the first bottom-gear engagement after a cold start was accompanied by an audible scrunch as a result of the relatively fast idling speed necessary to prevent stalling.

Ignition is controlled by a lever on the left side of the handlebar, though the lever is of the pattern normally used on the right side of a bar. After engagement of bottom gear on full retard, it was found desirable to advance the ignition partially or fully (by pulling the lever to the rear) before feeding in the clutch. For that reason a left-hand-pattern ignition lever would have

Information Panel

SPECIFICATION

ENGINE: 649 c.c. (71 × 82mm) overhead-valve vertical twin. Fully enclosed valve gear. Aluminium-alloy cylinder head. Light-alloy connecting rods; plain big-end bearings. Crankshaft supported in two ball bearings. Compression ratio: 8.5 to 1. Dry-sump lubrication; oil-tank capacity, 6 pints.

CARBURETTOR: Amal Monobloc with twistgrip throttle control; air slide operated by lever situated under seat. Air filter.

IGNITION and LIGHTING: Lucas magneto with manual control. Separate 60-watt Lucas dynamo and 6-volt, 12-ampere-hour battery. 7in-diameter headlamp with pre-focus light unit.

TRANSMISSION: Triumph four-speed gear box with positive-stop foot control. Gear ratios: bottom, 11.2 to 1; second, 7.75 to 1; third, 5.45 to 1; top, 4.57 to 1. Multi-plate clutch with Neolangite insert operating in oil. Primary chain, ⅜ × 0.305in in oil-bath case. Rear chain, ⅝ × ⅜in lubricated by bleed from primary chaincase; guard over top run. Engine r.p.m. at 30 m.p.h. in top gear, 1,760.

FUEL CAPACITY: 4 gallons.

TYRES: Dunlop: front, 3.25 × 19in with ribbed tread; rear, 3.50 × 19in Universal.

BRAKES: 7in-diameter rear; 8in-diameter front with ventilating scoops; finger adjusters.

SUSPENSION: Triumph telescopic front fork with hydraulic damping. Pivoted-fork rear springing employing coil springs and hydraulic damping; three-position adjustment for load.

WHEELBASE: 57in unladen. Ground clearance, 5in unladen.

SEAT: Triumph Twinseat; unladen height, 31in.

WEIGHT: 420 lb fully equipped, with full oil tank and approximately one gallon of petrol.

PRICE: £214; with purchase tax (in Great Britain only), £265 7s 3d. Extras: quickly detachable rear wheel, £3 (p.t., 14s 5d); prop stand, 15s 6d (p.t., 3s 9d); pillion footrests, 16s (p.t., 3s 11d).

ROAD TAX: £3 15s a year; £1 0s 8d a quarter.

MAKERS: Triumph Engineering Co., Ltd., Meriden Works, Allesley, Coventry.

DESCRIPTION: "The Motor Cycle", 27 October 1955.

PERFORMANCE DATA

MEAN MAXIMUM SPEED: Bottom: * 51 m.p.h.
Second: * 73 m.p.h.
Third: 94 m.p.h.
Top: 101 m.p.h.
*Valve float occurring.

HIGHEST ONE-WAY SPEED: 109 m.p.h. (conditions: strong near-tail wind; rider wearing two-piece riding suit and overboots).

MEAN ACCELERATION:

	10-30 m.p.h.	20-40 m.p.h.	30-50 m.p.h.
Bottom	2 sec.	2.8 sec.	2.8 sec.
Second	3.2 sec.	3 sec.	2.4 sec.
Third	—	4.6 sec.	4.6 sec.
Top	—	6 sec.	6.4 sec.

Mean speed at end of quarter-mile from rest: 82 m.p.h.
Mean time to cover standing quarter-mile: 16 sec.

PETROL CONSUMPTION: At 30 m.p.h., 100 m.p.g. At 40 m.p.h., 92 m.p.g. At 50 m.p.h., 80 m.p.g. At 60 m.p.h., 70 m.p.g.

BRAKING: From 30 m.p.h. to rest, 33ft (surface, dry tarmac).

TURNING CIRCLE: 14ft 6in.

MINIMUM NON-SNATCH SPEED: 18 m.p.h. in top gear with ignition fully retarded.

WEIGHT PER C.C.: 0.65 lb.

A ribbed drum and ventilation scoops are features of the 8in-diameter front brake. Stopping power was excellent

been preferred so that it could be pushed forward with the left thumb for advance while the clutch lever was still grasped.

Though temperatures below freezing point were frequently experienced during the test, engine starting was nearly always achieved at the first kick. Naturally, a vigorous thrust on the kick-start was necessary to spin the engine over compression. Prerequisites for cold starting were half retard, closure of the air lever, liberal flooding of the carburettor and a small (but not critical) throttle opening. Because of the very cold weather it was found necessary to leave the air lever closed or partially closed for the first mile or so. Situated beneath the seat, the lever was not too easy to operate with thickly gloved fingers.

Except for the common fault of a longish reach to the clutch and front-brake levers, all the other controls were quite convenient to operate and were smooth in action. (When a chain link was fitted between the lever and pivot-block of both the clutch and front-brake controls to reduce the reach required, there was still an ample range of lever movement.) The clutch was sweet yet firm in taking up the drive, and the gear pedal was pleasantly light to operate. Upward gear changes required a leisurely movement of the pedal if the dogs were to engage noiselessly. Provided engine speed was appropriately increased by slight blipping of the throttle, clean downward changes could be achieved without any pause in control movement. No difficulty was experienced in selecting neutral from bottom or second gear whether the machine was moving or at rest.

The riding position proved to be very comfortable for low and medium speeds. There was ample room on the dual-seat for a pillion passenger, though the width of the seat between the passenger's thighs was slightly too great to permit him comfortably to place his feet as far inboard on the rests as was desired. For sustained high-speed cruising, particularly against a strong wind, a position giving a more forward inclination to the rider's body would have been preferred in order to lessen the tension

in his arms caused by wind pressure. Strapping luggage across the dual-seat to support the base of the rider's spine proved helpful in this connection.

As is characteristic of modern Triumph twins, steering and general handling were extremely light. This trait, coupled with the armchair riding position and the machine's smooth response to the controls, made the T110 particularly delightful to ride at speeds up to say, a mile a minute. Confidence was soon engendered and stylish riding became automatic. Stability on wet city streets was first class. Unusually little effort was needed to heel the model over and, in consequence, it could be ridden round slow- and medium-speed bends in very slick fashion. At high speeds a greater degree of heaviness in the steering would have been appreciated, especially on bumpy road surfaces and in strong, gusty winds. In such circumstances a turn or two of the steering damper had a marked steadying effect on the steering, but was by no means essential.

Both front and rear springing were distinctly firm, a feature not uncommon on high-speed machines. As a result of the firmness no components fouled the ground when the model was banked steeply on corners; that was the case whether the machine was ridden one-up with the rear springing at its softest setting or with a pillion passenger and the springing adujstment at its hardest.

Matching the machine's speed capabilities, braking efficiency was higher than the relevant figure in the performance data suggests. The reason is that the front brake was more effective at high speeds than at 30 m.p.h. Even from near-maximum speed, firm application of the brake easily evoked a squeal of protest from the tyre. Leverage in the rear-brake control was high; consequently pedal travel was longer than average and the wheel could readily be locked. After dark, main-road cruising speeds of 60 to 70 m.p.h. were possible by the light of the headlamp beam.

As a result of the extensive full-throttle riding involved when compiling the performance figures, an appreciable amount of oil leaked past the gear-box mainshaft on to the rear tyre. Also when performance data were being obtained the ammeter failed, possibly as a result of vibration. When the machine was ridden in London traffic in particularly heavy rain, some misfiring was caused by water finding its way inside the sparking-plug covers. Long main-road journeys in similar weather, however, were quite free from the bother. The firm action of the taper-cock petrol taps was appreciated (the left-hand tap controls the reserve supply), as was the fact that four gallons of fuel could be put in the tank after a few miles had been covered on reserve. Both petrol and oil tanks have large, quick-action filler caps.

With its shell-blue and black finish, the Tiger 110 is extremely smart in appearance. Possessing a performance which suggests the analogy of an iron hand in a velvet glove, it is one of the most impressive Triumphs yet produced and is justly popular among sporting riders.

Though possessing exhilarating road performance, the T110 is not unhappy in heavy traffic. The manual ignition control can be used to obtain docile engine behaviour, while manœuvrability is very good

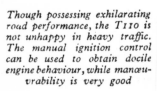

490 c.c. Triumph Speed Twin

Compact and Stylish Roadster, Light for its Engine Size, Lively yet very Tractable

By DAVID DIXON

PROBABLY no designer in motor-cycle history, I mused, has displayed a greater aptitude for being unorthodox without being irrational. In 1937 Edward Turner designed a vertical twin that looked like a single and set a world vogue. Now he has produced two machines—also twins—that are futuristic yet not so much so as to cause concern in conservative British eyes. The new 490 c.c. Speed Twin, to all intents and purposes identical except for engine size with the already established Twenty-One, has all the attributes one expects from a Triumph and more. It is a machine combining the weight of a lightish three-fifty with true five-hundred performance. And its lines are so sleek that the model can be thoroughly clean after ten or 15 minutes' leisurely work with a bucket of water, a sponge and a wash leather.

Just as the first Speed Twin stirred pulses some 21 years ago, so, beyond doubt, will the new 5TA excite comment the world over. Bore and stroke are 69×65.5mm. Crankcase and gear box are so formed that the engine basement can be worked on without disturbing the gear-box internals and vice versa. No five-hundred engine and gear box could be more compact. That feature—compactness—is characteristic of the entire machine. Wheel diameter is 17in, and the saddle height is 28½in when the machine is unladen and the rear-suspension units are in their lowest setting. The result is that riders of even shortish build can plant their feet squarely on the ground when they are astride the machine—an attribute much appreciated in these days of large-movement suspension systems.

Some may look on that saddle-height figure with a stony eye. But it should not be assumed for a moment that the riding position is cramped. With the footrests at their lowest setting (i.e., when the right-hand rest was down on the exhaust pipe) my long legs remained comfortable even on long journeys.

The gear pedal and brake pedal could be comfortably positioned in relation to their respective footrests but I was surprised to find that the left-hand side panel had to be removed before a spanner could be used on the brake-pedal adjuster. Initially the kick-starter crank fouled my right ankle, but turning the crank back slightly on its serrated shaft—a minute's work—set matters right.

SPECIFICATION

ENGINE: Triumph 490 c.c. (69×65.5mm) overhead-valve parallel twin; light-alloy cylinder head; thin-wall, steel-backed big-end bearings; crankshaft supported in ball and copper-lead bearings. Compression ratio, 7 to 1.

CARBURETTOR: Amal Monobloc type 375/75 with fabric-type air filter.

TRANSMISSION: Four-speed gear box in unit with the engine and driven by a ¾×⅜in duplex chain through a multi-plate clutch with Neolangite friction material and incorporating a vane-and-rubber shock absorber. Gear ratios: top, 4.8 to 1; third, 5.62 to 1; second, 8.35 to 1; bottom, 11.56 to 1. Final drive by ½×⅜in chain.

BRAKES: 7in diameter front and rear.

SUSPENSION: Telescopic front fork with two-way hydraulic damping. Pivoted rear fork controlled by Girling spring units incorporating hydraulic damping.

WHEELS and TYRES: 17in diameter wheels with straight-pull spokes and full-width, cast-iron front hub. Dunlop tyres, ribbed 3.25in front, Universal 3.50in rear.

ELECTRICAL EQUIPMENT: Lucas RM13/15 A.C. generator with emergency-start switching. Coil-ignition. Lucas 7in-diameter head-lamp with double-filament, pre-focus main bulb and pilot bulb; stop-and-tail lamp. Lucas 6-volt 12-ampere-hour battery.

FUEL CAPACITY: 3½ gallons.

OIL CAPACITY: 5 pints.

DIMENSIONS: Wheelbase, 52in; ground clearance, 5in; seat height, 28½in; dry weight, 350 lb.

PRICE: £245 15s 2d including British purchase tax.

MANUFACTURERS: Triumph Engineering Co., Ltd., Meriden Works, Allesley, Coventry.

In typical Triumph fashion, the control layout is commendably neat. The knurled cable adjusters in the clutch and front-brake pivot blocks gained full marks. The throttle cable adjuster, tucked out of sight in the tank's forward recess, did not. Neither did the lighting switch: mounted on the right of the nacelle, it had to be operated by the throttle hand. The combined dip switch and horn button are conveniently close to the left grip.

When the Triumph was collected, only 500 miles showed on the speedometer, so I decided to tread lightly for the next few hundred miles. But I need hardly have bothered. Out of traffic and on the open road the model revelled in whistling along at 60 to 65 m.p.h. At those speeds the exhaust was a pleasant, muted drone and no mechanical noise was apparent. Acceleration right up the scale was clean and impressive to boot, yet the engine was perfectly happy in top gear at 25 m.p.h. No longer, it seems, can the tag buzz box be applied to all oversquare power units. The degree of engine tractability is quite surprising. Maximum speed? Let's say that the machine will clock 85 m.p.h. comfortably and beat that speed if you squeeze it. On ordinary premium-grade petrol there was at no time the slightest trace of pinking. Except for a slight seep of oil from the indicator button, the engine remained clean.

Provided the carburettor air slide was lowered—it is actuated by a spring-loaded, cranked lever atop the instrument—and the float tickler lightly depressed, cold starting was faultless. The engine would not accept its normal mixture right away and hence it was better to let it run for a few seconds with the air slide in operation before moving off; the cranked lever is not easily found, given the necessary quarter of a turn and raised by a heavily gloved hand. Starting when the power unit was warm demanded no more than a gentle prod on the kick-starter. Ignition is by coil, with the current supplied by a Lucas alternator mounted on the crankshaft. An emergency position is provided so that the engine can be started even if the battery is flat; in this case the engine would fire only if the machine were push-started.

The high all-round performance achieved is not at the cost of economy. During 600 miles of give-and-take going on which I made a check, the consumption worked out at 75 m.p.g. (So the light weight, allied with the smallish frontal area, pays off in those directions, too.) During that period the oil level dropped a shade but a pint restored the level to its original height.

Although the design of the gear box differs considerably from that of the earlier Speed Twin the gear change is very similar. Pedal movement is slightly greater, perhaps, but it remains as delightfully light as always. Upward changes required a slight pause in pedal travel—especially between second and third—if truly silent dog engagement was to be achieved. Downward changes? They were made just as fast as the throttle, clutch and gear pedal could be manipulated! The indirect gears, especially third, were noisy.

Bonded Neolangite linings are employed for the clutch. Before starting from cold it was necessary to free the plates by depressing the kick-starter with the clutch lever pulled back in order to ensure quiet bottom-gear engagement. Operation was delightfully light and slip was never experienced.

Under normal conditions the Speed Twin's steering was characteristically light. Some may feel that, particularly on greasy surfaces, it is a shade too light to give a feeling of being truly positive. Straight-ahead steering, however, was true and negotiation of sharpish corners sheer delight. Heeling through traffic-free roundabouts was great fun. There appeared to be no limit to the angle to which the machine could be banked over. Long, sweeping bends could be treated as though they just weren't there. On bumpy surfaces the suspension gave the impression that the spring poundage—fore and aft—could be reduced with advantage.

The weather during the 1,000-mile test was far from good. There was drizzly and torrential rain, fog, sleet and high winds. First impressions—good as they were—were improved upon with almost every mile covered. Even in cross winds the Triumph gave no cause for concern. At first I had the impression that she shook her skirts excitedly as we crossed a side turning guiding a wind. But she quickly regained her composure.

Little else remains to be said of these 1,000 very pleasant miles. All Triumphs are well braked and the latest Speed Twin is no exception. That roll-on, levered stand is exemplary. The head-lamp beam was extremely shallow but sufficiently good to permit 60 m.p.h. cruising on the open road after dark. The prop stand holds the machine safely on even steep cambers and by means of the extension on its foot it can be easily operated. Ridden one-up, the twin-seat proved amply comfortable; two-up it was fine, too, provided the pillion rider did not attempt to sit far enough back to enable him or her to hold on to the strap attached to the seat's sides. Mudguarding? Let's say 99 marks out of 100.

Embedded in foam rubber under the seat, the tools are readily accessible. Battery, rectifier and coil are neatly grouped. The oil-tank filler cap is in the foreground

Such features as the finger-tip adjusters for the control cables, combined horn and dip switch and tank-top parcels grid are shown below

Straight off the Plinth

IT seemed downright indecent to take the Thunderbird off the platform. Radiating composure, grace and dignity, it stood alongside its several sisters—proudly displaying its new-look frame and styling and, like the others, was polished up to the eyebrows for the pleasure of the hundreds of Triumph dealers gathered at the factory last Thursday. Why indecent—haven't I long maintained that bikes are for riding, not ogling? And hadn't I gone along explicitly to gallop the 6T to London via Glasgow —a devious 720-mile route calculated to find out whether the new look was more than skin deep? True, but the first dozen miles of my run to Coventry in the morning had been covered in mist and the forecasters said it would return at dusk. Hardly fair on that spit and polish!

My concern was forgotten as chief engineer Charles Grandfield gave me details of the new steering layout. But had I known that in the next 48 hours the weather man was going to hurl the whole book at me, bar snow and ice, I might have changed my plans and enlisted with the spit-and-polish brigade. On torsion test, said Charles Grandfield, the new duplex frame (described and illustrated in last week's issue) has proved considerably stiffer than its predecessor, while the steering-head angle had been steepened

from 64½ to 67 degrees and fork trail increased. Wheelbase is 1½in shorter and, though no specific attempt was made to alter weight distribution, the shortening in effect brings the centre of gravity nearer the front wheel. By cutting down friction between fork springs and tubes, guides inside the springs improve sensitivity to small shocks; both front and rear damping are increased.

It was time to go in the late afternoon but just before I set off sales chief Neale Shilton applied some damping to my eagerness with the news that the 6T had been run for only half an hour on the rollers and 80 miles on the road—so would I please not gun it too hard at first?

I must say I liked the greater ease of straddling the model resulting from a reduction in wheel diameter from 19in to 18in. And though the Thunderbird exhaust note was never raucous, it was obvious from the start that it is even more subdued by the new mutes in the tail pipes. Preoccupied with thoughts of frames and steering geometry I vaguely sensed that the clutch lever was rather sluggish as I moved off. Only then did I remember that the

gear box had the Slickshift foot-change and I was delaying clutch engagement by easing my foot off the pedal too slowly. So I started changing without touching the clutch lever and was amused to see it come back to my knuckles of its own accord each time I stroked the pedal. After 20-odd years of conventional gear changing, I would not go out of my way to specify automatic clutch operation, especially with so much dense traffic to negotiate nowadays. But with precise co-ordination of throttle and gear pedal I was soon making quick, clean changes on the open road.

Determined not to exceed 65 m.p.h. on a whiff of throttle, I headed along A46 towards Leicester and soon found that the extra quietness of the 6T emphasized the smooth surge of power from lowish speeds: not the violent sort of power that seems to give you a rabbit-punch with each tweak of the grip, but certainly a deceptively close approach to it. As for the handling, it was far and away the best-steering Triumph I had ever ridden and comparable with the best on the road. True it would be many miles before I could try high speeds, but I felt really confident.

Approaching Newark, dusk called for the headlight and the pencil-slim main beam hit the road far too near the front wheel for my liking. A stop on A1 a little later would enable me to put

A north-south ride on the first

1960 Triumph Thunderbird

to leave the factory

By Vic Willoughby

Left: After the dealers' get-together at the factory, Vic Willoughby is seen off by the Editor, Harry Louis (middle) and Neale Shilton, Triumph's sales manager

that right, I thought, but I never got the chance. Soon I was groping my way through dense white fog and the low beam was, if anything, an advantage. For about 70 ghastly miles I thumbed my goggles incessantly, peered around for road markings and rang the changes between second gear and third. All very nice for the running-in but not for my enjoyment. With 138 miles notched up, Wetherby was quite far enough for that night; and after a welcome meal, I tilted the headlamp upward to the limit of the adjusting slots and swopped the dip-switch leads to give an up-for-main, down-for-dip action.

On flinging the bedroom window up next morning I was greeted with a murky view of the hotel car park—and the Triumph, like all the other vehicles, was dripping with moisture. Once out of town the headlight was essential and it would have been crass folly to top 60 m.p.h. even on the clearest stretches. A great deal of dual-road construction seemed to be going on though it was too foggy for me to judge progress. But it does seem that before very long the Great North Road will at last be worthy of its A1 designation. Nose to tail in gigantic convoys, the heavies were always quick to flash an invitation to pass, but single-track roads will be a thing of the past before a solo ceases to have an incalculable advantage in getting by.

At Scotch Corner the big hotel was practically hidden from view so that I nearly overshot the left fork, and once on A66 I had to cut speed down more still. By that time I was convinced that Neale Shilton was responsible for the fog—to ensure adequate restraint for the running-in, however throttle-happy I might feel! If it was a plot it failed; for as the Thunderbird swirled across the border into Westmorland, we ran into pale sunshine as suddenly as into fog the previous evening.

I was almost sorry at the change, for my right hand was itching and I had to use plenty of restraint to keep the 6T down to 70 per. But soon the sky was blue and the charm of the nearby hil-

At the top of the page the Thunderbird is seen on the plinth in the display hall at the Meriden factory before the trip

Backcloth to the 6T below is the 120-year-old Hamilton Mausoleum in Scotland. Built by the 10th Duke of Hamilton in the palace grounds, it was intended as a private chapel but proved unsuitable because of tremendous echoes. When the door is closed the sound reverberates for 15 seconds

Below: The author swings the Thunderbird into a slow left-hand corner. At all speeds steering was first class: the damper was nipped up only to stop the plates from chattering!

locks and the twisting, dipping road was recompense enough for the frustration. Shortly we were burbling over the red roads of Penrith, then gliding along the northernmost stretch of A6. And though I knew Carlisle of old, I would never have known how many pretty streets there are in its suburbs but for a tortuous diversion for through traffic.

By the time we ran into Crawford for lunch the Triumph was holding a steady 75 m.p.h. and on the open swervery to the north the precise steering gave me great fun. Shilton would have liked to see the 6T banking this way and that, but not the speedometer needle occasionally nudging 80—inadvertently, I swear.

Bellshill was my destination—the home of Joe Potts, Bob McIntyre's sponsor. Bob was away sunning himself on a well-earned Italian holiday, but Jim Fleming his mechanic, and I took a run out to Killearn hospital to see Alastair King, just transferred from Scarborough and only half a mile from home. Anyone who didn't know Alastair to be the livest of wires might have thought he preferred being abed—he was that cheerful. His

Mist darkened Wetherby last Friday morning. Once out of the town lights were necessary and speed had to be kept down for the next 60 miles

The top picture shows Joe Potts and Jim Fleming, respectively Bob McIntyre's sponsor and mechanic, getting the griff on the new-style Thunderbird from the author

Below: Night stop on the way to Scotland. The Angel Hotel in Wetherby is an old coaching inn, famous since the 17th century. Situated alongside A1, the hotel will have a quieter time when the town is bypassed by the new road to be opened next Monday

damaged arm is moving freely and by the time a double fracture of the left thigh is knitted, there should be nothing to hold up his return to full strength. It was a real pleasure to see him so lively.

Back at Bellshill it was early hours before Joe and I and Charlie Bruce (Scotland's fleetest two-fifty racer) gave up talking and crept off to bed. In readiness for the return trip I had topped up the Triumph tanks, tweaked the handlebar up so that the grips were horizontal and lowered the brake pedal a shade. Unfortunately that robbed me of a stop light, for with the pedal in the lower position the switch would not throw off. We tried to fake it and learned our lesson by burning out the battery lead in the process !

Within four miles of leaving Bellshill on roads drenched from overnight rain I was in trouble. As I notched top gear in Hamilton the nipple roller flipped out of the clutch lever and disappeared. Making getaways on the gear pedal was a clumsy business, but soon that difficulty was forgotten as the rains came. And how they came ! On two occasions flooded roads slowed me with a suddenness which brakes could never match. The back wheel spun easily in the lower gears as diesel drippings and mud reduced friction to that of wet soap. And the heavies raised almost impenetrable walls of blinding, stinging water. Bereft of visibility, comfort and clutch, I positively glowered at the border sign, "Haste ye back to Scotland."

Fortunately it was in Carlisle that it became obvious that gear-pedal starts were no match for dense traffic; Carlisle is the home town of the Tiffens, so I nipped round to my old friend Billy Tiffen, who produced a replacement roller—and a cup of tea. (To avoid a repetition of the loss, I decided to follow-through with my fingers on the clutch lever whenever I changed gear.) After I said cheerio to Billy the rain eased for a time, only to return with fresh vigour along the 50 miles from Penrith to Scotch Corner. There it eased again and soon, with 500 miles coming up on the clock, the Triumph was ploughing into a fair headwind at an indicated 75-80 m.p.h. At Brotherton, 205 miles from Bellshill, I had to switch on to reserve and the tank took just four gallons; that's the sort of range I like for long-distance touring.

On the way down to Newark there is some gorgeous open swervery and it was on that I learned that the new Triumph steers as precisely at 80 to 85 m.p.h. as at lower speeds. Handling was superb. The front suspension, too, matched up to the high criterion of being completely unobtrusive under just about all conditions. For my 10 stone though, the rear springing was decidedly hard ! It would perhaps ease off a trifle with more use.

On top of meals and refuelling, the bad weather and the delays meant that I finished my journey after dark and the headlamp beam was still a shade too much below horizontal. Anyway 70 m.p.h. was as fast as I felt happy, though I could no longer kid myself I was running-in the engine ! In fact, long spells of 80 to 85 m.p.h. in the afternoon told their tale when I went on to reserve little more than 180 miles beyond the lunch-time fill-up. Rather rapid running-in I fear, but needs must when time is short. In spite of the mist and rain it was an enjoyable and entertaining gallop, I felt, as I wheeled the Thunderbird into my garage on Saturday evening. The six-fifty engine gives silky power, and plenty of it, throughout the range, the brakes are excellent and the model certainly has eye-appeal. The last point is important to some riders but if, like me, you are more concerned with your mount's behaviour than its looks let me stress again that the duplex frame combined with the new steering layout and modified fork put the Triumph right in the top class for handling.

Built for·Speed No. 22

JOHN GRIFFITH describes the

GRE

The

which

to Fin

IN BRIEF

Engine : Parallel-twin o.h.v.; *either* 63 mm. bore × 80 mm. stroke=498 c.c. (9.5:1 c.r.); or 71 mm. bore × 82 mm. stroke= 649 c.c. (8.5:1 c.r.); no b.h.p. figures available; peak r.p.m. 7,600-7,800 on 500 c.c., 7,500 on 650 c.c.

Fuel Tank : Glass fibre, 2½ or 6 gal. capacity according to circuit.

Oil Tank : Glass fibre, 13 pt. capacity, 1 gal. use.

Wheels : Light-alloy rims carrying Dunlop racing tyres, 3.00-in. × 18-in. front, 4.00-in. × 16-in. rear, 3.50-in. × 12-in. sidecar.

Weight : 650 c.c., 350 lb.; 500 c.c., 340 lb.

BY far the most exciting duel for a place in the entire 1959 T.T. series was that fought out for sixth berth in the sidecar race between O. E. Greenwood on his Triumph-powered "special" and L. Neussner on a B.M.W.

At the end of the ninth lap Greenwood had let Neussner by in the mistaken belief that this was Schneider, the race leader, lapping him! He fought to overcome his disadvantage in a wheel-to-wheel battle throughout the ultimate lap, but did not succeed in getting past the German until Bedstead Corner—a left-hander where the B.M.W.. with its right-hand chair, was at

a theoretical advantage—less than a mile from the finish. At Governor's, Greenwood had a short lead, but the superior power of the B.M.W. enabled it to catch the Triumph, the outfits finishing almost abreast with the German some 15 m.p.h. faster— but on the line, where it mattered, the Triumph still had a few inches advantage!

What is this "special" that managed to head all the Nortons and several B.M.W.s? There is nothing revolutionary about it— just sound engineering and carefully applied common sense, as I found when I visited Owen Greenwood at his Thurmaston, Leicester, home to see his handiwork.

Two engines are available. For Grands Prix, where the capacity limit is 500 c.c., a 498 c.c. Triumph "Tiger 100" twin is fitted; for other events, which means most of the races in this country, a 649 c.c. "Tiger 110" unit is employed. The latter was installed when I saw the outfit, and is shown in the illustrations. The main external difference between the two is that a standard cast-iron barrel is used on the "650," whereas the "500" has its standard die-cast alloy muff with steel liners. Both engines are of current pattern with splayed-inlet, twin-carburetter heads.

Work carried out on the motors includes much polishing of moving parts, lightening

(Left) With the cowling removed this shows the fuel pump mounted on the timing cover of the 650 c.c. engine. It feeds petrol to a weir-type float chamber, surplus draining back to the tank by gravity. Note also the ultra-low position of footrest and gear change lever.

(Right) Much weight-saving has been effected by clever design of sidecar connections which rely on very small welded-on gussets to give the required support. The clutch also reveals painstaking weight-saving work ; the gearbox is a standard, close-ratio Triumph one except for a little more cutting and filing.

OD-TRIUMPH
INATION

ewed "Special"
First British Outfit
e 1959 Sidecar T.T.

Bird's-eye view of the engine shows how the frame tubes have been splayed to give adequate clearance. Note the strengthening gussets at the steering-head and the supports for the curburetter bell-mouths.

Add holes—add lightness.

the rockers and timing wheels and "altering the cams." Patient detail work on the engines over a fair period of time, says Owen, has resulted in a useful increase in top-end performance without any loss of bottom-end power.

The inlet valves have been trimmed to give a slightly narrower-than-standard seating surface so that they do not obstruct the incoming charge. Big-ends are plain Vandervell shell bearings, whilst ball thrust bearings are employed for driving and timing side mains. Ignition is by Lucas racing magneto and carburation by twin Amal GP10 instruments, with bore sizes of 1 3/32 in. and 1 3/16 in. on the small and big engines respectively. The fuel used is B.P. 100-octane and the oil B.P. R20, castor-base.

In an endeavour (so far successful) to avoid fracture, the exhaust pipes are fitted to the frame by Jubilee clips, instead of welded-on brackets, and to the engine by finned alloy rings which are ex-Rudge "Ulster."

Interesting is the fuel supply system. A pump mounted on the timing chest raises petrol from the tank in the nose of the sidecar to a home-brewed weir-type float chamber. Externally this is a normal-looking component with a feed into the top. The fuel passes down an internal tube, which almost touches the base of the chamber and then overflows, after filling a larger diameter tube attached to the base of the float chamber, to an outer section whence it drains back to the tank. Sectioned in plan, the chamber would consist of three concentric rings, with fuel fed into the centre one, taken to the mixing chambers from the next, and returning to the tank from the outermost of the three.

The maze of pipes all add to confusion, but the float chamber works very well. The carburetters and chamber are all rubber-mounted, the instruments being attached to the ports by rubber hose.

Transmission is via a Triumph close-ratio gearbox and a standard clutch with Ferodo inserts. The fact that Owen saved 2¼ lb. from the internals of the gearbox without altering any critical parts is indicative of the care he puts into his machine—and of the importance he attaches to weight saving.

The main frame was designed, and the tubes bent up by Ernie Walker and subsequently brazed by Owen himself. The swing-

ing fork is another Walker component. This year it pivots on Silentbloc bushes, as the bronze bushes used last year tended to wear excessively.

Front forks are cut-down "Manx" Norton and the wheel hubs are of similar origin. One advantage of the frame design is that the Triumph motor can be lifted straight out through the top tubes, after undoing the reamer-fitted engine bolts and the ancillary fittings.

The sidecar chassis was made by Don Houghton to his and Owen's design. It is exceedingly light and is attached to the bike by the simplest of connections. Small ears brazed to sidecar and machine tubes are joined by telescopic struts with strengthened, flattened ends—another weight-saving plan.

Three-millimetre plywood, suitably strutted, is used for floor covering—lightness again—but the main weight-saving device is the liberal use of glass fibre in the outfit. Sidecar body, sidecar mudguard, engine cowl, oil tank, fuel tank, seat-cum-tail-section and frontal fairing are all of this material. The fairing, complete with rev-counter and fittings, weighs only 15 lb.! Total weight of the complete outfit is almost 100 lb. lighter than an equivalent roadster solo.

Owen, with the help of passenger Terry Fairbrother, mechanics Bill Powell and Roger Campton and glass-fibre expert Dennis Nixon, hopes soon to complete a second outfit so that he will have a "500" for Grands Prix and can reserve the "650," with the increase in power, for home events. Until then he is pretty good at changing engines!

649 c.c. Triumph Bonneville 120

SPARKLING PERFORMANCE FROM THE LATEST VERSION OF A FAMOUS ROADBURNER

TRACTABLE POWER, SUPERB BRAKES AND GOOD ROADHOLDING *By DAVID DIXON*

I AM much too well bred ever to give the raspberry. But to those who chant that 100 m.p.h. motor cycles are noisy and intractable I give the nearest (well-bred) approach to the raspberry I can muster. My views on the subject have been mightily reinforced after a few days, mainly very wet days, spent on a 1961 Triumph Bonneville 120.

The era when performance at the top end of the scale was achieved to the detriment of poke at the other end is decidedly past. This mile-eater will span 80 m.p.h.—from 25 to 105 m.p.h.—in top gear. And what's more it achieves that nigh-incredible feat without fuss or coaxing. In weather more favourable than I had, that 105 m.p.h. figure, by the way, could be very handsomely bettered.

It was just my luck that such an exciting beastie should come along when rain, rain, rain, was the order of the week. More than my enthusiasm was in for a damping—or so I thought as I threw a leg over the Bonneville for the first time. But the model was as impatient as I to reach the wide open spaces, even if the roads were under water.

The Bonneville, it is true, will tick-tock along at 30 m.p.h. with the top cog in mesh, but this is no town runabout. As soon as the speed-limit signs are left behind, you drop down a ratio, or maybe two, and get to work on the right grip. Characteristically Triumph, power is on tap from the moment the grip is tweaked. There is no hesitancy, no fluffing. Those twin carburettors really do their stuff.

In bottom gear, in an almost alarmingly short time, the Bonneville will reach 50

m.p.h. A quick upward flick on the gear pedal and 70 m.p.h. shows. As third is snicked home there comes another beefy surge, 88-90 m.p.h. comes up and things begin to get exciting. Then top is engaged.

Wind pressure on a bulky, riding-coated, overtrousered and booted figure slows the rapid, forward tramp in the 94-95 m.p.h. region. A semi-crouch excites the speedometer again and the needle will teeter readily round the 105 m.p.h. mark.

On a dry, deserted road, with a two-piece-suited rider adopting a racing crouch, my guess is that it would be rela-

tively cushy to beat 110 or even 115 m.p.h. I am writing, incidentally, in terms of *indicated* speeds. There was no real opportunity to test the clock for accuracy. But I had no reason to believe it unduly optimistic.

Maximum speeds of the order of 110 m.p.h. are, of course, of little more than academic interest. A high, genuinely usable, cruising speed is of far more importance. Right then. Settle for 85 m.p.h.? That's chicken feed for this baby. Wherever road conditions permit, speeds of that order can be maintained without fuss. Farther up the scale a high-

Below left: The engine remained oiltight throughout. The folding kick-starter pedal rotates and the light switch is located beneath the seat. Right: Two Amal Monobloc carburettors are fitted as standard

rigid. The model is rock-steady at all speeds. There are few machines I would ride hands-off at 80-plus on wet, windy days and on greasy roads, but I had no qualms about doing so with the Bonneville.

Some slight effort was required to lay the machine into a corner; but once on line, it stayed there. In typical Triumph fashion the machine could be heeled well over until something grounded—the prop stand on the left or the footrest on the right.

Roundabouts were great fun and sinuous West Country roads even more so. In spite of its appearance, the Bonneville is not in the least top-heavy. It can be chucked around with all the abandon of an expert juggler pitching Indian clubs.

I would have preferred softer suspension. The spring poundage could with advantage be reduced. Both front and rear forks are well damped, although that up front is very sensitive to changes of temperature.

Initially, I thought the riding position rather cramped. But, after several hours of high-speed blasting, I had a complete change of heart. It is just right for the job. Reasonably short and flat, the handlebar gives just the right degree of forward lean for counteracting wind pressure. And the rear of the three-gallon tank is narrow, affording excellent knee grip.

On any high-speed roadster, powerful braking is of vital importance. A Triumph modification for 1961 allows the shoes to float, and the linings are resited round towards the trailing ends of the shoes. The result is impressive to say the least.

Cheeks creased by wind pressure, David Dixon and the Bonneville crack along at 80-plus near Runnymede. Below: The new front brake in its full-width hub incorporates floating shoes and improved lining location

frequency tremor at the handlebar can be felt—a tremor that is present also at equivalent engine speeds in the indirect ratios. It disappears at 100 m.p.h.

So the machine is a flyer. What is sacrificed for performance? Tractability? Not a bit. Pulling away from a standstill can be accomplished as readily on the 8.25 to 1 second gear as in the 11.92 to 1 bottom ratio. Noise? The most grumpy of grumpy silence-please addicts couldn't complain of that.

The performance, then, is fully usable without objection. True, there is some mechanical noise from the valve gear but that wouldn't trouble anyone but the most fastidious perfectionist. Thirst? Overall fuel consumption was about 52 m.p.g.

Those twin carburettors needed careful synchronization for slow idling, but, at best, idling was not always completely reliable. Another mild snag with twin carburettors is that twistgrip operation is somewhat heavier than it is with a single instrument. But these are minor debits in such a glowing balance sheet.

Provided the carburettors were flooded, first-prod starting was the rule even after the model had spent a night in the November open. Quite a bit of muscle is required, by the way, to bump the engine over compression—the ratio is 8.5 to 1.

To stifle any tendency toward pinking, 100-octane petrol was used throughout. I ran out of fuel on one occasion. Believe it or not, this magnificent motor cycle has no reserve tap.

The gear box lived fully up to the Triumph reputation. Pedal movement is up for upward changes and down for down. Gear selection is rapid and noiseless, though, between second and third, a slight pause in pedal travel is essential. The new clutch friction material employed effectively eliminates sticking plates. There is no longer any need even to free the plates before the first start of the day. Provided the engine was idling slowly, bottom gear could be noiselessly engaged. Pleasantly light in operation, the clutch took up the drive smoothly and without snatch.

For assessing roadholding and handling I could hardly have chosen worse conditions. On one 400-mile run I had only some 50 miles of dry road. It is all the more credit to the model, then, that I at no time had the least cause for anxiety. Yet *average* speeds most of the time were in the mid-fifties.

Steering is considerably heavier than that of previous Triumphs, and considerably improved by being more positive. Torsionally, the duplex frame is extremely

Light in operation, both brakes were extremely powerful and—an excellent feature—they were unaffected by water.

The chromium-plated headlamp takes one back to the days of pre-war Triumphs. There is no nacelle—and, as on the Trophy models, the headlamp unit is quickly detachable; the wiring harness is connected to a quick-release multi-pin plug behind the lamp. Adequate power

for 60-65 m.p.h. cruising was provided by the headlamp beam. The light switch is located beneath the dual-seat (with the best of intentions, no doubt), but how are you supposed to reach it when you are on the move? Giving a quick flash from pilot to main beam for overtaking is impossible. No marks for that one.

I liked the sporty appearance of the narrow mudguards but they are hardly suitable for wet-weather riding. Another detail criticism is that the steering-damper knob repeatedly unscrewed. My only other point concerns the oil filler cap; when can we have one that doesn't seep oil?

Outweighing these criticisms by a long chalk are detail features to appeal to any enthusiast. The control cables, for example, have cam adjusters at the handle-bar ends. That roll-on centre stand really does its stuff. Twistgrip friction is easily adjusted by means of a spring-loaded screw with knurled knob. The throttle-cable adjuster is readily accessible.

That, then, is the Bonneville 120 as I found it. It is a machine that is very, very fast, and, with its excellent handling and superb brakes, safe to ride almost irrespective of the conditions. It may not be quite so tractable as some, but there is nothing about its power and torque characteristics to render it in the least unsuitable for town work. In fact, in any company, this latest Bonneville is an absolute honey, with no vices—and attributes by the score.

Above: Built primarily for the purpose of defeating time, the Bonneville is acceptably orthodox in appearance

Left: The flat handle-bar aids high-speed motoring and the ball-end control levers are there to comply with competition requirements. The tank top grid saves the paint-work when carrying luggage

Old and new. The Bonneville may not be built like Windsor Castle but it enhances the entrance setting

SPECIFICATION

ENGINE: Triumph 649 c.c. (71 x 82mm). overhead-valve parallel twin; plain big-end bearings; crankshaft supported in two ball bearings. Light-alloy cylinder head; cast-iron cylinder block; compression ratio, 8.5 to 1.

CARBURETTORS: Two Amal Monobloc; no air slides.

ELECTRICAL EQUIPMENT: Lucas RM 13/15 alternator charging 6-volt, 12-ampere-hour battery through rectifier. Quickly detachable Lucas 7in-diameter pre-focus headlamp with 30/24-watt main bulb and integral pilot light. Lucas magneto ignition with auto-advance.

TRANSMISSION: Triumph four-speed gear box driven by ½ x 0.305in chain through multi-plate clutch with bonded friction faces. Gear ratios: top, 4.88 to 1; third, 5.81 to 1; second, 8.25 to 1; bottom, 11.92 to 1. Final drive by ⅝ x ⅜in chain.

SUSPENSION: Triumph telescopic front fork with two-way hydraulic damping. Pivoted rear fork controlled by adjustable Girling spring units incorporating hydraulic damping.

TYRES: Dunlop 3.25 x 19in ribbed front and 4.00 x 18in Universal rear.

BRAKES: 8in-diameter front; 7in-diameter rear.

FUEL CAPACITY: 3 gallons.

OIL CAPACITY: 5 pints.

DIMENSIONS: Wheelbase, 56½in; ground clearance, 5in unladen; seat height, 31in; weight, 403 lb with about one gallon of petrol and full oil tank.

PRICE: £288 5s 11d (including £49 5s 11d British purchase tax). Extras: Quickly detachable rear wheel, £3 16s; prop stand, 19s 11d; pillion footrests, 19s 11d; steering lock, 13s 3d.

MANUFACTURERS: Triumph Engineering Co., Ltd., Meriden Works, Allesley, Coventry.

ROAD TESTS OF NEW MODELS

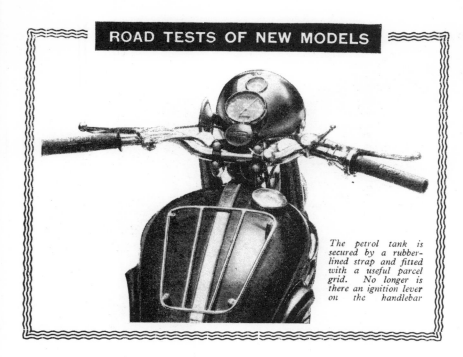

The petrol tank is secured by a rubber-lined strap and fitted with a useful parcel grid. No longer is there an ignition lever on the handlebar

ing power and by the extremely happy gearing. so that there was as much joy in wafting the Trophy up and down the speed scale in top gear as in using the indirect gears to the full.

So widespread a feature is overgearing that on first acquaintance the Triumph seemed to be undergeared. The impression soon gave way to wholehearted approval, however; for not only did maximum speed prove to correspond with the peak-power r.p.m. of 6,500, which is as it should be. but the availability of the full engine-speed range in top gear made for extreme flexibility and liveliness.

From about 45 m.p.h. in top gear acceleration was decidedly brisk, and around 65 m.p.h. the Trophy was really into its stride. With the twistgrip about two-thirds open 85 m.p.h. could be held indefinitely on long runs, while tweaking the grip fully could be relied on to send the speedometer needle round to the 95 m.p.h. mark, still with the rider normally seated.

The top gear speeds shown in the performance panel were obtained without the rider wearing waterproof kit. Full plastic and rubber wet-weather gear reduced the figures by some 3 m.p.h. Its needle prone to flutter a shade at high speeds, the

649 c.c. Triumph Trophy TR6

FOUR models offering various shades of performance and refinement comprise the Triumph B range. All are six-fifty twins. For riders with extreme tastes the choice is easy: the skirted, low-compression Thunderbird for the tourist; the naked, twin-carburettor Bonneville for the out-and-out sportsman.

And for riders with broader tastes? For them the single-carburettor Trophy TR6, restricted to overseas sales for the first half of the year, is reintroduced to the home market. In the degree to which it combines tractability and unobtrusiveness with sheer zip and stamina the Trophy reaches a very high standard indeed. It will exceed 100 m.p.h. with acceleration to match, yet it is comfortable, quiet and very well mannered in dense traffic.

You may look at it either way. The Trophy provides practically all the urge of the Bonneville without the slight twist-grip heaviness that comes from working two throttles, the initial need to synchronize the carburettors for idling, the periodic call for balancing the throttle-cable settings for a really sweet take-off, and without the extra thirst of a two-carburettor engine. Or you may think of the Trophy as virtually, but not strictly, a Tiger 110 (the high-performance version of the Thunderbird) without the partial rear enclosure.

In fact, the TR6 shares not only the Bonneville's naked frame and gaitered, heavy duty front fork, but also its 4.00 ×

18in rear and 3.25 × 19in front tyres, sports mudguards, three-gallon petrol tank, quickly detachable headlamp and lower gearing (4.89 to 1 top as against 4.67 for the other six-fifties). Like the T110, however, it has a less hairy inlet camshaft and an air filter, though retaining the Bonneville's 8.5 to 1 compression ratio.

In keeping with the recent trend in sports machines, auto-advance is employed on the Trophy—and it works faultlessly. Super - premium petrol was generally used and it was just about impossible to make the engine pink, whatever the load or treatment. The resulting sweetness was enhanced by an unusually wide range of lusty pull-

Outboard of each exhaust port the cylinder head fins are joined by a cast-in buttress

speedometer had a maximum error of about 3 m.p.h. (fast) which occurred at 40 m.p.h., 70 m.p.h. and top speed.

When a pillion passenger was carried there was, of course, more incentive to use the gear box to the full; the best pick-up was obtained by changing up at 40,

60 and 85 m.p.h. For the most part the exhaust note was quite inoffensive; but the Trophy lacks the well known Triumph mutes in the tail pipes and harsh acceleration in bottom gear gave rise to a rather flat note.

At high speeds some engine vibration was perceptible, especially if the petrol tank was gripped between the knees, but the tremor was always tolerable and never set a limit to cruising speed.

Extremely good compression on both cylinders and a high kick-starter ratio combined to provide a good deal of resistance to the folding pedal for starting. However, following the normal drill, the first vigorous thrust with the rider's weight behind it never failed to bring the engine to life. Idling was reasonably slow, though the temptation to seek a gas-engine tickover led to an occasional tendency for the engine to cut without warning.

The latest clutch friction material entirely eliminates the old Triumph bother of the plates sticking overnight. There was never any call to free the plates before starting the engine, and invariably the first gear engagement of the day was noiseless. Once the transmission had warmed up, however, bottom gear more often than not went home with a light click.

Drive take-up was sweet and firm and there was never any suggestion that the clutch was getting unduly warm, even

after a succession of full-throttle getaways. As with most Triumph gear boxes, really clean changes called for a rather deliberate pedal movement when changing up and an appreciable blip of the throttle when going down—especially between second and third gears.

Nominally, bottom gear may seem a shade on the high side at 11.93 to 1. But the ease with which the Trophy restarted on M.I.R.A.'s 1 in 3 test hill proved the ratio to be by no means too high; and it certainly makes the gear more than usually useful.

On congested city roads the Trophy had precious few vices. The 90-degree elbow where the throttle cable leaves the twistgrip made it impossible to achieve as much control delicacy as would have been liked just off tickover setting. And the siting of the main light switch beneath the seat nose is anything but convenient. But both engine and transmission work smoothly at 30 m.p.h. in top gear, and by and large the Trophy is well-nigh as pleasant to ride in town as on the open road.

As delivered, the riding position proved fine for medium-size riders, though those with longer legs might prefer to lower the footrests a shade. The passenger's position is equally comfortable and the twin-seat abundantly roomy.

Though they have an ample range of deflection, both front and rear suspension proved decidedly firm; pitching was never

experienced solo and only very mildly two-up. Provided the bulk of the cornering effort was applied through the knees rather than the hands, bend swinging was precise and exhilarating. And so long as the rear suspension units were set correctly for the load carried (using the C-spanner provided in the tool kit) the machine could be cranked over hard without fear of serious grounding.

When forcing the Trophy round high-speed bumpy curves it paid to balance the pull on both handgrips if a slight wobble was to be avoided; but the steering damper was never brought into serious use —merely tightened enough to prevent it from vibrating undone.

The headlamp switch is situated just beneath the seat nose on the right-hand side

✻ ✻

In keeping with its sparkling all-round performance, the Trophy TR6 has a gay appearance

For competition work the headlamp may be removed in a jiffy after pulling out the wiring plug

Good as it unquestionably is, the 30ft 6in stopping figure shown in the performance panel fails to do full justice to the brakes. The self-servo action of the floating shoes, with their asymmetrical linings, gives instantaneous, smooth and powerful braking from the highest speeds; and only light pressure is needed on the controls, though not so light as to cause the slightest qualm in wet weather.

After many hundred miles of hard riding, the engine remained commendably free from oil seepage. But a dribble of oil escaped from the tank filler cap when maximum revs were sustained, as when taking the full-throttle performance figures. If the rear chain was not to run dry on the one hand or the wheel and tyre not to pick up too much oil on the other, the setting of the bleed from the primary chaincase had to be adjusted very precisely. A few degrees less than a quarter turn out was found best on the test model.

At all but the lowest speeds the horn note was insufficiently effective, but the lights were of average power, i.e. good enough for moderately high speeds. However, a more secure location for the detachable plug in the headlamp socket is called for; no matter how carefully the plug was fitted it vibrated out in time.

Since the Trophy petrol tank has a nominal capacity of only three gallons, it was a surprise to find that it would comfortably accept 3½ gallons once the reserve tap was brought into use. Incidentally, the plastic coating of the taper cocks gives the taps an extremely sweet action with absolute freedom from sticking and leakage.

Both prop and centre stands have accessible extensions and provide sound support. Downward pressure on the centre-stand footpiece takes a great deal of effort out of bringing the stand into use. The toolkit is adequate for routine maintenance and, with the exception of primary chain adjustment, all the tasks are straightforward. To obviate the possibility of the gear box skewing under load, a drawbolt is fitted at each side; but the left-side bolt is so closely flanked by a rear engine plate and the primary chaincase as to make the adjuster and lock nut difficult to turn.

Smartly finished in ruby red and silver with plenty of black enamel, chromium plating and polished light alloy, the Trophy drew praise even from non-motor cyclists for its gay appearance. Which is just one more reason why it is a machine one cannot fail to take pride in.

Specification

ENGINE: Triumph 649 c.c. (71 x 82mm) overhead-valve parallel twin. Crankshaft supported in two ball bearings; plain thin-wall big-end bearings. Light-alloy cylinder head; compression ratio, 8.5 to 1. Dry-sump lubrication; oil-tank capacity, 5 pints.

CARBURETTOR: Amal Monobloc with air filter. Air slide operated by handlebar lever. Spring-loaded friction adjuster on twistgrip.

IGNITION and LIGHTING: Lucas magneto with auto-advance. Lucas RM 13/15 alternator with rotor mounted on left end of crankshaft, charging six-volt, 12-amp-hour battery through rectifier. Quickly detachable, chromium-plated, 7in-diameter headlamp with pre-focus light unit.

TRANSMISSION: Triumph four-speed gear box with needle-roller layshaft bearings. Gear ratios: bottom, 11 93 to 1; second, 8.27 to 1; third, 5.82 to 1; top, 4.89 to 1. Multi-plate clutch with cork-base friction facings running in oil. Primary chain, ½ x 0.305in in cast-aluminium oil-bath case. Rear chain, ⅝ x ⅜in with guard over top run and lubricated by adjustable bleed from primary chaincase. Engine r.p.m. at 30 m.p.h. in top gear, 1,900.

FUEL CAPACITY: 3 gallons.

TYRES: Dunlop; front 3.25 x 19in ribbed; rear 4.00 x 18in Universal.

BRAKES: 8in-diameter front, 7in diameter rear, both with floating shoes and finger adjusters.

SUSPENSION: Triumph telescopic front fork with hydraulic damping and dust-excluding gaiters. Pivoted rear fork controlled by Girling spring-and-hydraulic units with three-position adjustment for load.

WHEELBASE: 56in unladen. Ground clearance, 5½in unladen.

SEAT: Triumph twin-seat; unladen height, 30½in.

WEIGHT: 400 lb fully equipped, with full oil tank and approximately one gallon of petrol.

PRICE: £229; with purchase tax (in Great Britain only), £276 4s 8d. Extras: Pillion footrests, 16s 6d (p.t., 3s 5d); prop stand, 16s 6d (p.t., 3s 5d).

ROAD TAX: £4 10s a year; £1 13s for four months.

MAKERS: Triumph Engineering Co., Ltd., Meriden Works, Allesley, Coventry.

PERFORMANCE DATA
(Obtained at the Motor Industry Research Association proving ground at Lindley, Leicestershire.)

MEAN MAXIMUM SPEED: Bottom: *48 m.p.h.
Second: *70 m.p.h.
Third: 95 m.p.h.
Top: 101 m.p.h.
*Valve float occurring.

HIGHEST ONE-WAY SPEED: 105 m.p.h. (conditions: moderate following wind; rider lightly clad).

MEAN ACCELERATION:

			10-30 m.p.h.	20-40 m.p.h.	30-50 m p.h.
Bottom	...	...	2.1 sec	2.0 sec	—
Second	...	...	3.0 sec	2.9 sec	2.5 sec
Third	...	...	—	4.2 sec	3.4 sec
Top	..	...	—	5.7 sec	4.5 sec

Mean speed at end of quarter-mile from rest: 87 m.p.h.
Mean time to cover standing quarter-mile: 15.1 sec.

PETROL CONSUMPTION: At 30 m.p.h., 102 m.p.g.; at 40 m.p.h., 93 m.p.g.; at 50 m.p.h. 81 m.p.g.; at 60 m.p.h., 68 m.p.g.

BRAKING: From 30 m.p.h. to rest, 30ft 6in (surface, dry tarmac).

TURNING CIRCLE: 16ft 8in.

MINIMUM NON-SNATCH SPEED: 20 m.p.h. in top gear.

WEIGHT PER C.C.: 0.62 lb.

See this Triumph powered world-beater at Earls Court

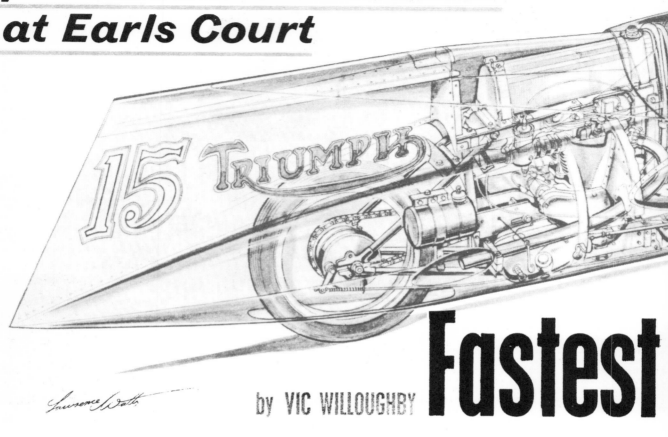

Lawrence Watts

by VIC WILLOUGHBY

Fastest

IN a projectile measuring 17ft from nose to tail you would imagine there would be plenty of room for the rider. But that's not so with Joe Dudek's red and white Triumph-powered streamliner. Rider Bill Johnson is as slim as they come. Yet the light-alloy monocoque cockpit fits him as closely as his underwear. A course of muscle building and he'd be in trouble.

Elbow width is a bare 20in. The most Spartan wire padding keeps his backside only 3in off the Utah salt, while the quick-release glass-fibre cockpit cover grazes the top of his helmet. Three small clear-plastic panels give him a view to the front and sides. A lap strap fastens him down. To cushion the kick of acceleration, backrest and headrest are thinly padded.

Between the rider's knees is a vertical column, at the top of which is pivoted the handlebar. The ends are bent down very steeply and measure just 15in across. Steering lock is limited to a few degrees. The clutch lever on the left is fitted upside down so that it points skyward. More unusual still, a front-brake lever is used instead of a twistgrip to operate the throttles. (There is no front brake.)

When changing gear Johnson drops his right hand straight off the bar on to the positive-stop lever on the side of the cockpit. A similar lever on the left releases the spring-loaded struts that project from behind the seat to support the machine when it comes to a standstill.

Other cockpit controls are a lever on the right-hand side connected to the fuel cock, a magneto switch on the steering column and a rear-brake pedal on the centre line, where it can be operated by either foot or both. In a panel directly above the steering column is the rev-meter.

Basically, Dudek's streamliner can be considered in three parts. The 4ft-long cockpit is the middle part and there is light-alloy bulkhead at each end of it.

Bolted to the front bulkhead are two tubular triangles bridged at the forward apex by a cross tube carrying the front wheel. Made from an obsolete Triumph rear spring hub, this wheel incorporates hub-centre steering. Pin-jointed track rods pass back through the bulkhead to the handlebar.

The 19in steel rim carries a ribbed Dunlop Track Racing tyre with a tread depth of only 1mm (0.040in). There is no springing front or rear.

At the front, the reinforced aluminium-alloy shell is cone shape, blending at the cockpit to cylindrical with a tunnel along the top to fair the rev-meter panel and merge with the cockpit cover. On the underside of the nose a divided spat deflects air away from the front-wheel opening to pre-

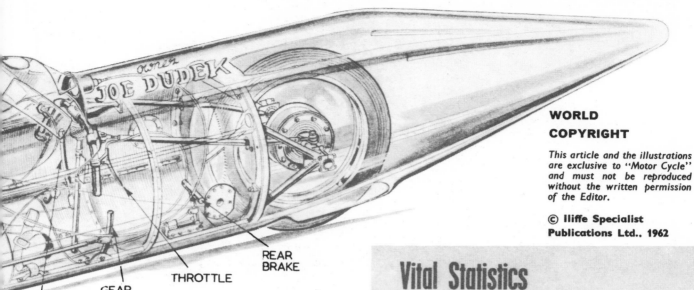

STRUT
RELEASE

GEAR
CHANGE

THROTTLE

REAR
BRAKE

Vital Statistics

Height: tail fin 37in, canopy 34in, cockpit tunnel 27in, nose 12in. Wheelbase 96in. Weight 400 lb. Length 17 ft. Width 20in. World's record 224.57 m.p.h. American ditto 230.07 m.p.h. Fastest run 236 m.p.h. Most hectic run— blown off course by side wind at 230 m.p.h.

Motor Cycle

COPYRIGHT

machine on earth

vent pressure from building up inside and lifting the nose.

The shell has more affinity to supersonic rocket practice than for the streamline shapes usually used for subsonic speeds (i.e., below 750 m.p.h.).

Behind the rear bulkhead is a structure made of steel tubing, light-alloy plate and angle strip. Besides housing the Bonneville engine, gear box and rear wheel, this structure incorporates a safety roll loop behind the headrest.

The fuel tank sits above the engine, the oil tank alongside the rear wheel. That has a light-alloy rim and a tyre of the same size and pattern as the front.

Access to the engine is gained though hinged doors in both sides of the fairing. Scoops in these doors lead air to the

cylinder block. The rear half of the block is closely cowled to circulate the air through the fins.

With a compression ratio of 11 to 1, the engine breathes alcohol vapour through two massive hose-mounted Amal racing carburettors fed by a float chamber between them. Tract length from carb mouth to valve head is 12in. Thirty-three inches long and $1\frac{1}{2}$in in diameter, the plain exhaust pipes discharge through cut-aways in the shell sides. Ignition is by a Lucas racing magneto.

A small hole in the fairing alongside the gear box allows a kick-starter to be inserted! Not so strange when you realize that top gear is about $2\frac{1}{2}$ to 1, and so bottom is just over 6 to 1— hardly the ratio for push-starting.

Bill Johnson, who piloted the cigar-shape projectile for both the American and world records.

GUNNING A NEW-

Vic Willoughby grabs a Triumph 1963 prototype and burns a tankful of juice in a hurry

IT was a long time since I had covered so many miles on end at over a ton. And, strangely enough, the previous occasion was also on a Bonneville. (That was two years ago when chief tester Percy Tait and I shared a Thruxton-trim model for five one-hour stints on the Motor Industry Research Association's banked triangle, to average some 111 m.p.h.)

But last week's mount was in roadster trim—a 1963 proto-type (with new frame and integral crankcase and gear box) snatched with some difficulty from Percy and development engineer Doug Hele.

My arrival interrupted intense steering developments and so the engine, said Doug, was a run-of-the-mill affair. Some mill! So long as I sat up, respectable-like, with my feet on the front pegs, the job would hum along with the speedo needle a notch or two beyond the 100 mark.

Whenever I shifted by boots to the pillion rests and chinned the tank-top luggage grid another ten knots were rung up on the dial. So commonplace did this sort of gait become on M1 that, when I eased the grip, 90 m.p.h. seemed slow and 80 a dawdle.

But however saturated with speed my senses became, there was always an ample safety margin. For moderate pressure on the brakes would dip the nose down hard and kill the speed as quickly and safely as if I'd run into a glue patch.

Trusting a rev-meter more than a speedo for accuracy, I first asked Doug about the engine's limits. Its peak of 46 b.h.p., he told me, is given off at 6,500 to 7,000 r.p.m. (That range is equivalent to 102-110 m.p.h. in top, so overall gearing is spot-on.) The danger zone for valve gear is 7,500 r.p.m. upward.

Unfortunately the revmeter betrayed me by going haywire, so in the lower three gears I had to rely on my ears and the speedometer. A shade below 50 and 70 m.p.h. seemed ample in bottom and second. Indeed, for the best sort of get-up-and-go, upward gear changes were made some 5 m.p.h. below these speeds.

Which is not surprising, since the higher figures mean 7,500 r.p.m. where engine power is already tumbling down the far side of the graph.

In third, 90-odd m.p.h. seemed the obvious speed for notching up. Agreed, says the slide-rule—7,000 r.p.m.

PICK-UP!

Full-bore acceleration in bottom gives a very convincing answer to why so many sprint stars prefer a Bonneville engine. That pick-up is legalized violence.

From any normal speed in second and third throttle response is surging. Indeed, from as low as 40 m.p.h. in top the Bonnie will gather itself together in a most workmanlike fashion.

But in top gear it is at 80 m.p.h.—when the average sixfifty is working quite hard—that the Bonneville engine gets its lungs full and starts to repay years of painstaking development.

STEERING

At the other end of the scale the engine was not able to show its best British manners. For it was equipped with American-market energy transfer ignition. Drawback with that is the narrow range of automatic timing (12 deg). As a result, full retard is 26 degrees before top dead centre, which makes idling fast.

For all that I trickled smoothly through tiny villages at 30 m.p.h. in top cog. The early timing on retard showed up most in an occasional kick back when starting and the inevitable scrunch that accompanies bottom gear selection at a fast tickover.

(The seemingly peculiar American choice stems from their use of Bonnevilles almost exclusively for sport rather than transport. They prefer to dispense with a battery and

are prepared to tolerate the e.t.'s meagre 18 watts for lighting. Ugh!)

All right—so you want to know about the steering. Well, with Doug Hele's long experience at Nortons, I wasn't surprised to find him going all out to put Bonneville handling on the topmost pedestal. And it's odds-on he'll have done it by the time the models get to the customers.

Already fork trail has been increased to stop the front end flapping on full-speed bumps. Several times when flat out I hit patchy road repairs without a waver. But occasionally at 100 m.p.h. upward I found a trace of the old weaving. The attack on this problem is already under way.

Doug Hele's coldly logical approach would confound

SPECIFICATION

ENGINE: Triumph 649 c.c. (71 x 82mm) overhead-valve parallel twin; plain big-end bearings; crankshaft supported in two ball bearings. Light-alloy cylinder head; compression ratio. 8.5 to 1.

CARBURETTORS: Two 1 1/16 in-bore Amal Monoblocs.

ELECTRICAL EQUIPMENT (for home market): Coil ignition. Lucas RM 19 alternator charging 6-volt, 12-amp-hour battery through rectifier. Lucas chromium-plated 7in-diameter pre-focus light unit with quickly detachable, multi-pin plug-and-socket connection.

TRANSMISSION: Triumph four-speed gear box driven by ⅜in-duplex primary chain through multi-plate clutch with bonded friction facings. Gear ratios: top, 4.84 to 1; third, 5.76 to 1; second, 8.17 to 1; bottom, 11.81 to 1. Final drive by ⅝ x ⅜in chain.

SUSPENSION: Triumph telescopic front fork with hydraulic damping. Pivoted rear fork controlled by Girling adjustable spring-and-hydraulic struts.

WHEELS and TYRES: 18in-diameter wheels; full-width front hub. Dunlop tyres: 3.25in front, 3.50in rear.

BRAKES: 8in-diameter front, 7in-diameter rear with floating shoes.

TANK CAPACITIES: Petrol 4 gallons, oil 5 pints.

PRICE: £318 including British purchase tax. Extras: pillion footrests, £1 4s; rev-meter, £7 16s.

MANUFACTURERS: Triumph Engineering Co. Ltd., Meriden Works, Allesley, Coventry.

LOOK BONNIE

Unit construction, latest frame and restyled tank give the 1963 Bonneville fresh lines

ON THE ROUGH

by PETER FRASER

Missing Five-hundreds

Latest Bonneville cylinder head has greater fin area and ribbed rocker boxes; spring-steel tabs secure the inspection caps. The two Monobloc carburettors are widely splayed. Petrol taps are lever type (without reserve). Access to the contact breaker entails only removal of the round cap in the timing cover

WHAT happened at the Lancs Grand National? There was not a single five-hundred in the first three in any of the races. For a national event of such status this was surely a sorry state of affairs.

If it arose because the A.C.U. 500 c.c. Scrambles Star had already been won by Jeff Smith (who was at the Southern Trial), then some thought ought to be given to the matter when next year's calendar is being planned. With the Lancs falling at the end of the season, the same thing could recur annually—to the detriment of this magnificent event.

Too Easy

I HAVE RECENTLY been discussing the ease with which it is possible to obtain a national competition licence. At the moment the licence amounts to no more than a receipt for a ten-shilling fee to the A.C.U. for entering your name on a register. I am by no means alone in feeling that a simple qualification (such as an open-to-centre first-class award, or a place in a junior race at a scramble) is long overdue.

Profitable

FEW PEOPLE appear to stop to think that if a trials course is sufficiently severe to sort out the Millers and Smiths, it is likely to be beyond the ability of a novice. Yet who gets the blame if some misguided novice gets stuck in a section and causes a lengthy delay? The organizer for sure! At scrambles, too, one sees riders, obviously outclassed, being lapped by faster men before a third of the race is over. I would be the last to question the enthusiasm of novice competitors. But I have some doubts about the system which permits them to compete on level terms with experts. Perhaps the licences issued, now topping the 4,000 mark annually, provide too useful a source of revenue for the established scheme to be altered?

Here's How

THERE STILL seems to be a little doubt how points are amassed in order to qualify for the British Experts Trial, which takes place on Saturday, November 24. A win in any of the qualifying events is worth 20, runner-up ten, then seven, five, four and three for the remainder of the first six places. Sidecars score 20, seven and four for the first three places. The list comprises all A.C.U. national trials. the Scottish, Valente. Coronation, Hurst, Hallamshire Peak and Inter-Centre Team trials. Irish riders who finished in the first six in the M.C.U.I. Inter-club championship—and anyone who has won the Experts in the past five years also qualifies. This month the event moves back to Ludlow. A two-lap course totals 70 miles and includes 110 sub-sections for solos and 72 for sidecars.

COMPETING in the North Berks Club's time-and-observation trial on the Sunday before last I noticed that a little over half the entry were wearing helmets. Those who had scrambled, ridden in the International or were regular road men, wore them. Trials riders who never ride a machine other than in an event did not.

BRIAN MARTIN, B.S.A. competitions manager, tells me that the factory will be supporting Jeff Smith and Arthur Lampkin in next year's 500 c.c. world moto-cross championship series. The pair will be mounted on B40 - type machines. Jeff, it will be remembered, set the moto-cross world talking when he won on a B40 in Sweden this year.

many a clubroom boffin. You can set too much store, says Doug, on whether a frame loop is single or duplex—and he instances the Navigator and Dominator Nortons to make his point.

He applauds the stiffening of the rear-fork pivot on the new frame. But his chief aim now is to keep the front wheel glued to the deck, for it is only then that the castor action due to fork trail can exert its stabilizing effect on steering.

RUBBER INSULATION

My space is running short, so let me condense some random impressions. Twist-grip action was delightfully sweet and light in spite of there being two carburettors. Equally silky is the scissors action of the new clutch control mechanism. And the bigger clutch hub rubbers,

resulting from the change from four- to three-vane transmission shock absorber, do a good damping job.

Riding position made me feel at home and the slimmer, deeper tank shape is a decided improvement. Width across the thin rubber kneepads is very comfortable. The footrests could be grounded only on low- and medium-speed corners.

The experimental fork top yoke did not have the 1963 rubber mountings for the handlebar. And though the tremor at the grips was tolerable, rubber insulation would have cut down the occasional need to take a fresh handful of twistgrip.

After I'd burned my quickest tankful of juice outside M.I.R.A. I could find no oil leaks. What if the exhaust pipes had the blues? I certainly hadn't!

FIRST Triumph twin to employ unit construction of engine and gear box (apart from a wartime model of which few were built) was the 348 cc 3TA of 1957. Two years later came the corresponding 490 cc 5TA, but the Meriden six-fifties retained a separate gear box until the introduction of the 1963 range.

Those pre-1963 bigsters have already been dealt with in this service series. Though most of the following hints concern the unit-construction models only, a few will apply equally to both types of machine.

UNIT-CONSTRUCTION TRIUMPH TWINS

SERVICE-SHOP LORE NUMBER TWENTY-FIVE

BLOWN FUSE

FOR THE past year, all twins have incorporated a replaceable fuse between battery positive terminal and earth. Initially, this was of 25-amp rating but a change has now been made to 35-amp.

Should the fuse blow, use a 35-amp replacement, no matter which type was fitted originally.

Because there would no longer be a constant voltage supply from the battery, a blown fuse can give the effect of a false ignition retard— and, indeed, symptoms that indicate engine seizure.

Should the bike misbehave in this way, don't get alarmed. Check the fuse first; it may be nothing more than that.

(One customer actually sent his machine all the way back to the factory by rail, convinced that the pistons had packed up! A glance at the fuse would have saved him the trouble.)

TWIN CONTACT BREAKER

STUMBLING-BLOCK for many riders is the setting of the contact-breaker points gaps. They go to consider-able trouble to equalize the two gaps, then find that the engine doesn't run smoothly.

However, it is *not* essential for the gaps to be equal. Correct procedure is as follows.

First, set each gap to a nominal 0.015in opening— but note that this must be done when the points have just been fully opened by the cam. The reason for this pre-caution is that should there be any eccentricity in the cam or spindle, further rotation would alter the points gap.

Set each gap independently, of course, rotating the engine shaft as required.

Now slacken the screws securing the contact-breaker back plate and rotate the plate slightly until the points just start to open when the piston reaches the specified position.

For the 3TA and 5TA, this is 0.010in (six degrees) before top dead centre; for the TR6 and Bonneville, $\frac{1}{16}$in before tdc; for the Thunderbird, $\frac{1}{32}$in.

Time the point of opening correctly on one piston, then rotate the engine shaft one complete revolution; the second set of points should now be starting to open.

If they are a fraction out— and this is the important bit

grip each tongue, in turn, in the jaws of a vice and squeeze gently. This should spread the metal outward enough to compensate for the wear.

Note the word is " gently "; a few thou should be quite enough, and the plates must remain free to slide in the shrouded slots of the clutch drum without binding.

FUEL TANK
(Six-Fifties)

WHEN removing the fuel tank from a Thunderbird, or any other six-fifty equipped with nacelle headlamp, you may find that the top of the tank fouls the underside of the nacelle unit.

Don't strain it, or you will scratch the tank paintwork.

Instead, extract the two securing screws at the rear of the nacelle. There will then be sufficient clearance for the tank to come away without bother.

still—by sliding a length of rubber tubing (a piece of bicycle tube, for instance) over each rod.

Don't forget to unwrap the rods when the engine is being re-assembled!

BATTERY MOUNTING

UNLESS the securing strap is kept tight, with the rubber buffer in its correct position under the strap, the battery could vibrate up and down in its carrier.

The oil-return pipe passes alongside the battery, and this movement of the battery can result in the pipe chafing a hole in the casing.

SPEEDO DRIVE

IF A THUNDERBIRD, Trophy or Bonneville is to be used for sidecar work it will be necessary, in addition to lower-

ing the gear ratios, to change the speedometer drive gears in the gear box, employing a 9-and-15-tooth set instead of the standard 10-and-15-tooth pinions.

Note that though one pinion is 15-tooth in each case, they are *not* dimensionally alike.

Any other change—for instance, to a close-ratio gear cluster or to a smaller rear wheel—would involve replacement of the speedometer head.

Ask the Triumph service department for a copy of Bulletin No 11 in this connection.

REPLACING GUIDES

VALVE GUIDES are of sintered iron and could break up if hammered severely. Great care is therefore needed when fitting replacement guides to a cylinder head.

Best dodge is to pop the new guides into the freezer

Below right: Rotating the contact-breaker backplate, after slackening the fixing screws, to get the lower set of contacts just breaking

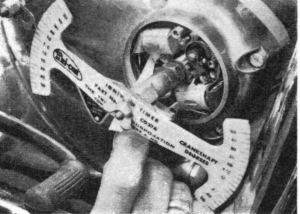

Right: Using a timing device, marked in crankshaft degrees, to get spot-on ignition timing. A pointer is attached using a convenient timing-case screw hole

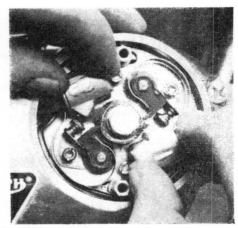

If this fuse blows, the symptoms can indicate engine seizure! Note that the battery retaining strap must be kept tight and the rubber buffer under it must be in position

—it is quite permissible to alter the gap on that side to, say, 0.013 or 0.017in, to bring the point of opening to the correct position.

Current twins already embody a means of finding top dead centre rapidly. In conjunction with this, Triumphs will soon be marketing a plastic timing disc which can be attached by the contact-breaker securing bolt.

CLUTCH RATTLE

USUAL cause of clutch rattle is wear on the tongues of the friction plates. In this case,

CON-ROD PROTECTION

TOO MANY owners, having stripped off the cylinder block and pistons, allow the connecting rods to drop against the crankcase mouth.

These rods are of light alloy and, if allowed to flap about in this way, could be nicked against the sharp edges of the mouth—and that is tantamount to inviting subsequent fracture at the point of the nick.

Give them some form of protection, either by wrapping them with several turns of insulating tape or—better

compartment of a domestic refrigerator for about half an hour.

Now put the cylinder head in the kitchen oven for about ten minutes on low heat until the metal is just too hot to touch.

(If Mum happens to be cooking dinner, a bucket of very hot water will serve almost as well.)

When the respective parts are withdrawn from the fridge and oven, you'll find the guides will almost fall into place, and may need nothing more than a light tap, using a wooden drift.

ROCKER-BOX LEAK

SHOULD an oil leak develop between the base flange of the rocker box and the top of the cylinder head, which cannot be cured by fitting new gaskets, the base flange must be smoothed down to remove irregularities in the surface.

First, extract the two studs which project downward (this can be done easily, if two nuts are locked together on the stud).

Now spread a truly flat surface, such as a piece of plate glass, with fine grinding paste, or lay a sheet of fine emery cloth on the glass.

Lightly rub the flange on the paste or emery, using a circular motion and making sure that the flange is flat against the glass, until high spots are rubbed away.

Wash the surface with petrol to remove all traces of paste or emery powder before refitting.

EXHAUST CAMSHAFT (C Range)

ON C-RANGE models (that is, the 3TA, 5TA and Tigers 90 and 100) it is possible to extract the exhaust camshaft— to replace it with a high-performance shaft, for instance, or to gain access to the revmeter drive thimble at the far end of the shaft—without dismantling the engine to any extent.

Remove the cylinder head, and the exhaust pushrods and cover tube. Lift up the tappets and wedge a block of rubber between them to secure them in the raised position.

Now the camshaft gear can be detached, so giving access to the removable plate behind.

Turn the camshaft so that the cams are clear of the tappet feet—and simply pull it clear.

For added security on plug-in ignition and lighting switches, this hooked washer can be fitted, to take a rubber band as shown

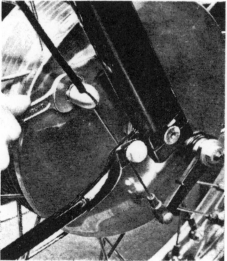

Slackening the shoe pivot spindle nut prior to applying the brake in order to centralize the brake shoes. The nut must be tightened while the brake is held hard on

Below: Squeezing the clutch-plate tongues. This will spread the metal sufficiently to take up the wear

PLUG-IN HARNESS

FOR THE past two or three years, the wiring harness of Triumph models has embodied a plug-and-socket connection to the underside of the main switch.

The harness plug is normally a firm fit in the switch socket. However, to prevent any chance of the connection coming adrift in use, recent machines have featured a metal clip secured between the top surface of the switch unit and the underside of the headlamp shell or nacelle, together with a rubber band which passes under the harness socket.

This clip and band can be fitted to earlier models very

simply (or an owner could make up a similar arrangement for himself). Part numbers are F5983 and F5988; —total cost is 2s 2d.

CENTRALIZING BRAKES

IT ISN'T generally realized that, on the Triumph front brake, the shoe pivot is rather smaller in diameter than the hole in the brake plate; this permits the shoes to be centralized, ensuring maximum area of contact between linings and drum.

Technique is to slacken the pivot spindle nut (on current models, this is also the brake-cable stop), then apply the brake hard. Keep it applied while you retighten the nut.

On the rear brake, the same principle applies, but here it is the central hole in the shoe plate which is made larger than the wheel spindle.

Slacken the shoe-plate lock-nut, apply the brake pedal and retighten the lock-nut.

POOR EARTH

LAMP BULBS which burn out persistently, or a low battery charging rate, can generally be traced to a poor earth somewhere in the electrical circuit.

The cause could be paint or rust preventing a good contact at the headlamp or tail-lamp mountings.

Check, too, the earth connection from the battery, and the mounting of the rectifier.

649 cc Triumph T120 Bonneville

The Bonneville as she was—the pre-unit-construction engine of reporter John Northover's bike

PARK a Bonneville and it will be immediately surrounded by the youthful enthusiasts of the district. They will gaze with awe at the prominent twin carburettors, admire its sporty lines. "What will she do, mate?"—that's the question you're most likely to be asked.

That is how 21-year-old Barry Oram, of RAF St Mawgan, sees the call of the Bonneville. And he is undoubtedly right. There *is* something about the T120. No doubt about it at all—and this is certainly the most appealing report I've had to write. Indeed, very few keen motor cyclists could fail to catch just a whiff of that special brand of enthusiasm which clings to the Bonneville as resolutely as does a be-pouched kangaroolet to its mum.

The Bonneville owner is the one who has taken a deep breath and inhaled oodles of this abundant enthusiasm.

Yet, surprisingly, considering the obvious keenness, only slightly over 90 owners sent in their reports (30 came from Triumph Owners' Club members).

Nevertheless, those who did write were typical T120 riders. The Bonneville man is a more clearly defined type than the owner of any other bike we have reported on.

He is 23 years old and he has notched up six years of riding since that first provisional licence. And what riding!

It is obvious that he doesn't regard his roadburner as solely a thing of beauty, to be polished and exhibited to admiring glances; *his* bike has to earn its keep to the tune of many thousands of hard miles every year.

Reporters, who averaged 16,000 miles on their present mounts, have covered nearly 1½-million miles between them.

Not adverse to a bit of a burn up, our enthusiastic Bonnieman has a preference for race-bred customizing.

Just harken to this typical list of mods (from 25-year-old Colin Wheeler of Liverpool): E3134-form cams and racing followers, racing valve springs, roller main bearings, chopped Monoblocs and remote float chamber, Peel Mountain Mile fairing, clip-ons, five-gallon glass-fibre fuel tank, twin-leading-shoe front brake with racing linings and, on occasions, a racing seat.

This is the Bonneville that most of the reporters would aspire to. Many, though, are too fond of regarding their 649 cc of searing docility as an all-rounder and, so, prefer to leave things standard.

The most succinct summing-up, and one that echoes the sentiments of nearly everyone, comes from 18-year-old Peter Nash of Birmingham.

"To me the Bonnie is a factory-built special and for road-burning it cannot be beaten. It stays in tune and takes a belting without protest."

And when they come to a

For fast road work there's nothing like a Bonnie. So enthuse our contributors. Here Mike Evans tries a 1964 mount borrowed from Elite Motors of Tooting

RIDERS' REPORTS
NUMBER NINE

Collated by MIKE EVANS

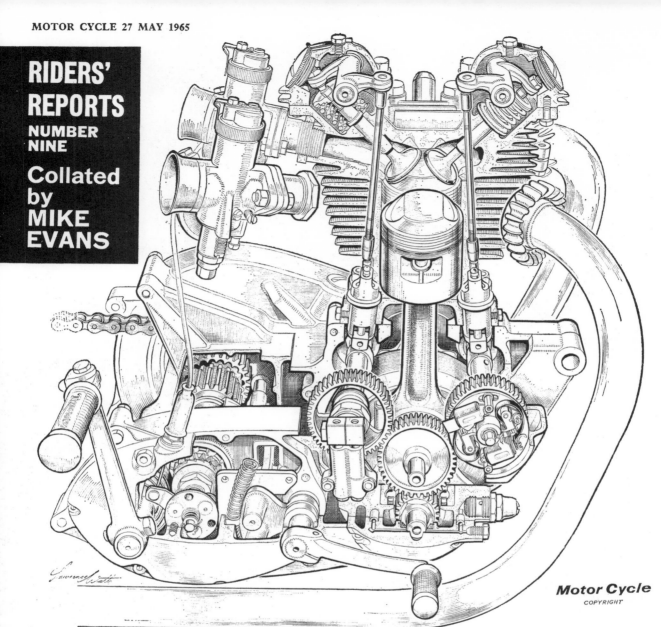

*I*nside gen. This engine-gear box unit came on the scene in October 1962—and it certainly tidied up the appearance of the Bonnie. Transfer of the contact breaker to the right-hand end of the exhaust camshaft further improves the appearance. Other interesting features include the high piston crowns (giving a compression ratio of 8.5 to 1), three-ball clutch operation and locking tabs for the valve covers

conclusion like that, reporters are thinking along quite logical lines. No one imagines that absolutely everything in the cabbage patch is green and healthy. But in the Bonneville's patch there's an abundance of green.

Performance

THIS title word is synonymous with Bonneville in the motor-cyclists' dictionary. "Performance is what I bought the bike for—and I've had my money's worth." That's the verdict of Alan Stanley, 20, of London.

"Best of both worlds," reports Barry Adams, Hull, Yorks. "It gives flexibility *and* speed. One can trickle along through town at 30 mph in top gear without the slightest bother and even accelerate from this speed without need to change into a lower ratio; yet, on the open road, scorching acceleration is available the moment the twistgrip is turned."

Alan Stanley gives an exciting account of a typical ride. "Hard acceleration has the front wheel skimming the surface of the road, and me hanging on. This continues up to about 85 mph, when the front

wheel settles on the tarmac."

"But the acceleration doesn't stop there. Change into top at 90, whack the throttle open and the bike leaps forward with the speedo needle swinging past the three-figure mark. For high-speed cruising the Bonnie's a dream—there's no vibration range at all."

Not everyone would agree with Alan's vibration-free mount being typical. There is no doubt from the letters that a number of Bonnevilles do have noticeable vibration periods—usually in the upper rev band.

Triumph Club member Francis Smith, age 53, of

Birmingham, is emphatic that he has never experienced the "turbo smoothness" one reads about in reports.

Ton-twenty? True or false? That is the question most often on the tips of non-Bonneville-owning tongues.

From the reports it is difficult to say. Most readers acknowledge their speedometers to be rather optimistic, and have made allowances for this in quoting their speed figures.

Average works out at 113 mph—which is pretty good. Only one or two claim 120 mph as genuine, but many say that 125 mph can be seen on

The dream bike of all our contributors, the 1965 version of Triumph's most famous roadburner. Note especially the ultra-clean lines of this modern unit-construction six-fifty power unit

Right: Reporters like the way the seat hinges up to reveal the battery, oil tank and tool roll

the clock occasionally; this they refuse to believe.

Cruising speed? About ninety, reports Colin Wheeler. However, he warns that you should beware bits falling off if that speed is maintained for any length of time.

Starting

DEFINITELY reliable. First or second kick even in winter. With no air slides fitted, the float chambers must be well flooded.

Fuel Consumption

"AMAZING for a twin-carburettor machine of this tune," enthuses Leslie Looker, 21, of Stratford, East London. "I get nearly 100 mpg below 40 mph and have hardly ever had less than 70 mpg in mixed town and open-road going."

However, on an average basis, the Bonnie is not quite so economical. Sixty mpg seems a good all-rounder.

Doubts about sobriety come from 28-year-old girl rider Kirsten Peschel of Copenhagen: "I can only say it is a fast drinker."

Handling

AH, THOUGHT I, quietly, there'll be fun here. But no. Reporters in general were busy a-burying bogies as quickly as they could dig them to mind.

Rear-end whips? Hinged frame? Fact?

No. "Roadholding," says Peter Nash, "is above average. Gone are the days of the rattle-snake, as Triumphs were called around Birmingham. True, the rockers on my 1960 model still rattle, but the snake has unobtrusively curled up and gone to sleep."

Most attribute the Triumph's evil reputation to earlier models—especially those fitted with sprung hubs.

Barry Oram gives a balanced view: "The Bonnie is no perfect roadholder (what machine is?); the main trouble comes on long, fast bends where a good maxim is to keep the power on, particularly when negotiating a sub-standard surface.

"Anyone who rolls back the grip on an 80-mph bend without good reason deserves whatever any machine may do."

Confirms 22-year-old Colin Agate, of Wallington; "Road-holding of my 1963 Bonnie is miles better than that of my 1962 duplex-frame Trophy and as good as my friend's 650SS."

Electrics

IF COLIN AGATE, as he says, had no trouble, he is in a minority.

With 23,000 Bonneville miles to his credit, 24-year-old Michael Warne of Abbots Langley, Herts, concedes that the lighting is adequate—when working. His machine

Here's the Triumph engine with the mostest—most go and most owner-appeal. It breathes through twin Amal carburettors and packs a punch of 46 bhp at 6,500 rpm

PERCENTAGE VOTE

■ AFTER sending in their reports, readers were asked to complete a questionnaire in which they answered specific questions according to the formula good, middling or poor.

In calculating these figures we have allowed two points for good and one point for middling. Poor got nothing.

THE MARKS ARE GIVEN AS PERCENTAGES

Acceleration	100	Accessibility	76	Workmanship	90
Flexibility	85	Steering	85	Quality of Finish	82
Smoothness	80	Suspension (front)	85	Lighting	50
Starting	88	Suspension (rear)	87	Horn	16
Oil-tightness	81	Smoothness of		Other Electrics	54
Reliability	91	controls	88	Tool Kit	64
Clutch	90	Riding Position	93	Spares from	
Gear Box	80	Brakes	79	Factory	70
Delivery Tune*	83	Mudguarding	45	Spares from Dealer	70

*Secondhand machines not taken into account

Is the machine a good buy? 99 per cent say yes.
Would you buy another Triumph? 90 per cent say yes.
OVERALL MARK (average of the above percentages): 76.48 per cent.

ALL ABOUT THE BONNIE

THE Triumph Bonneville is such an indispensable part of the motorcycling scene that it seems impossible it was introduced as recently as October 1958. It climbed to the heights of popularity immediately and has remained there ever since.

Triumphs originated the vertical twin as we know it today. Before the war their twins were almost an oddity in a world of lolloping, big singles and monster vee-twins.

It was during the life of the Bonneville that the Triumph twin was extensively revamped—its engine and gear box were joined in wedlock at the altar of unit construction. First unit Bonnie appeared for the 1963 season.

1965 SPECIFICATION

ENGINE: Triumph 649 cc (71 x 82mm) overhead-valve parallel twin; plain big-end bearings; crankshaft supported in two ball bearings. Light-alloy cylinder head; compression ratio 8.5 to 1.

CARBURETTORS: Two 1⅛in-bore Amal Monoblocs.

ELECTRICAL EQUIPMENT: Coil ignition. Lucas alternator charging six-volt 12-amp-hour battery through rectifier. Quickly detachable Lucas chromium-plated 7in-diameter headlamp with pre-focus light unit.

TRANSMISSION: Triumph four-speed gear box driven by ⅜in-duplex primary chain through multi-plate clutch with bonded friction facings. Gear ratios: top, 4.84 to 1; third, 5.76 to 1; second, 8.17 to 1; bottom, 11.81 to 1. Final drive by ⅝ x ⅜in chain.

SUSPENSION: Triumph telescopic front fork with hydraulic damping. Pivoted rear fork controlled by Girling adjustable spring-and-hydraulic struts.

WHEELS and TYRES: 18in-diameter wheels; full width front hub. Dunlop tyres: 3.25in ribbed front, 3.50in rear.

BRAKES: 8in-diameter front, 7in-diameter rear, both with floating shoes.

TANK CAPACITIES: Petrol 4 gallons, oil 5 pints.

PRICE: £326 13s 3d.

MANUFACTURERS: Triumph Engineering Co, Ltd, Meriden Works, Allesley, Coventry.

---

has had every electrical item renewed at least once during his ownership.

Others are even less fortunate. Take Lawrence Gatehouse, a 22-year-old sales engineer of Newark. In four years' riding his Bonnie consumed 19 ammeters, five batteries, three rectifiers and two alternators.

Some have cured battery boiling problems—cause of short life—by changing over to 12-volt electrics.

Tales of replacements and trouble are too numerous to be coincidental. Take the three percentage marks covering the sparks side of the Bonnie: lights 50, horn 16 (a monotonously regular figure in these reports) and electrics in general, 54. Average of that

little lot is a very mean 40 per cent.

However, it should be said that most of the really gorey tales refer to pre-unit-construction jobs. The factory say that the current models are giving little trouble.

Indeed, if the unit-construction machines are considered apart from earlier models, the electrics receive a slightly better score of about 60 per cent.

Reliability

NINETY-ONE per cent is a very satisfactory mark for reliability. And the Triumph engine comes out with colours fluttering proudly atop the mast.

Immaculate 1961 pre-unit construction Bonnie. Schoolteacher John Northover, of Worthing, has done 40,000 miles on it

Says 24-year-old Barry Adams: "My 1962 mount has covered 37,000 miles and no major work has been called for on the machine. Indeed, the cylinder head has never been removed."

Once the carburettors are precisely set, he adds, they need little attention and give a reliable tickover.

Several readers make special mention of excessive primary chain wear—particularly noticed on the older non-unit construction jobs.

Blame for this rests with a leaky chaincase, they say.

Sufferers might find it better to dispense with the metered oil bleed to the rear chain (only on pre-1963 models). That way most of the oil stays in the primary chaincase and all you have to do is oil the rear chain in the normal way.

However, Colin Wheeler, of Liverpool, comes up with a real rib-tickler (not for him, of course): "Primary chain wear on my 1961 Bonnie is fantastic due, no doubt, to the patented Triumph total loss oil system of the primary chaincase.

"I am now on my fifth chain after only 35,000 miles. Also, when the oil vanishes from the chaincase, the chain stretches, whips about and clobbers the ac generator with disastrous results. I am now on my fifth generator (£8 a time). Is this a record?"

Really proud of his T120's reliability is 24-year-old schoolmaster, John Northover of Worthing.

"The Bonnie is incredible.

In the last 3½ years and 40,000 miles I have thrashed my bike mercilessly. It has been cruised for many, many thousands of miles at 80 mph plus, and driven at maximum speed on hundreds of occasions; yet it shows no signs of such a strenuous life."

He is so confident that it will not let him down on this year's 2,000-mile, continental trip that he volunteers to consume his Barbour mitts—wax 'n all—if it does!

Brakes

MIXED feelings here. With a mark of 79 per cent in the table, riders are just on the side of thinking their brakes good. (If everyone had reported "middling" the mark would have been 50 per cent.)

Says Barry Oram: "Brakes are sufficient for moderate riding and quite adequate for a Tiger Cub!"

Yet Alan Stanley thinks his stoppers really potent. "Hard pressure on the front brake has the fork bottoming and the tyre squealing."

More than a few enthusiasts discovered oval drums on their new Bonnies.

Transmission

CLUTCH action is quite adequate, report the majority —90 per cent in the table is creditable enough. But the gear box does attract a few brickbats.

"Long travel of the gear lever means that I can be sure of getting a positive change when belting the bike only by hooking up the lever.

"Trying to change with my foot still on the rest can produce a neutral between the gears or a scrunchy clonk on engagement." That's the opinion of one southern reader.

But there are others—as always—who have nothing but praise for the action of the box. Guiding light here must be the 80 per cent mark—quite a good showing.

Riding Comfort

"FOR ME the riding position is perfect and has not been altered since the day I got the bike. After three or four hours' fast riding I can dismount without an ache in my body," says Alan Stanley.

"Standard bars gave me backache on long runs so clip-ons and rearset footrests were fitted. They were found better all round, and still gave full lock." (Colin Agate).

Well, it takes all sorts. Basic fact is that the Bonneville is a comfortable bike—or, if you prefer a racier set up, you can convert it easily yourself.

Special praise is handed out to the large dual-seat.

Accessibility

NOT too bad for a modern twin, is the general opinion. Malcolm Fewings, 21, of Newport, Mon, says that accessibility is poor. Rockers have to be adjusted almost by guess work. Gear box drain and level plugs are hard to reach.

One or two points mentioned: it is necessary to take off the tank to adjust the rockers properly and to adjust the carburettor cables. Everyone is unanimous though that, on the whole, the engine is dead easy to work on.

Service

EVEN GROUPING HERE —70 per cent for both dealer and factory service. The particular moan of TOMCC member Stanley Branicki is that many dealers advertise Triumph spares down to the last item—but often enough they haven't got what you want.

However, another reader

Right: Full-width front hub on a 1960 job—a Bonnie feature praised by most contributors. Far right: Sporty, functional handle-bar layout; the revmeter is an optional extra. The characteristic Triumph luggage grid is well liked

says that spares are obtainable anywhere and they are in great abundance if you shop around instead of going to one or two shops.

Of dealers mentioned in letters, Harveys, Pride and Clarke and H and L come to mind readily. Many other smaller dealers are praised.

Response from the factory is usually prompt and kindly. Many have good Samaritan tales to recount—perhaps of how bikes were fixed outside the guarantee period because the factory felt it had a moral rather than a legal responsibility to do so.

In one or two cases long waits are mentioned—but it appears that Triumphs manage to be on the ball more often than they are off it.

Final word from Colin Agate: "Great—100 per cent every time, and cheap."

Overall View

"AN EXTREMELY comfortable and well-designed tourer, with sufficient docility for commuting and fast enough to acquit itself favourably against any production machine on the market.

"Reliability, economy and superb after-sales service combine to make this a much sought-after mount which I would not hesitate to recommend." Dave Thompson speaking.

Ken Nicholls, 58, of Blackheath, London, speaks from 35 years of riding experience. He finds the Bonnie a dream bike with few faults.

He averages 20,000 miles a year, does the minimum maintenance. But, like many other ardent Bonneville enthusiasts, he can see the other side of the picture:

"The faults are common to most bikes these days—lousy

horn, derisory sealed-beam light unit, dud batteries, absurdly unreliable switches, feebly designed rear-light attachment, poor chromium plate."

Only one or two are really bitter about the Bonneville. Malcolm Fewings has had enough trouble to last him a life-time with his 1964 model —in only 3,500 miles. He is obviously unlucky.

Whatever the trials, most can see the attraction of a searing sportster really shining through.

The Bonnie inspires enthusiasm. When 24-year-old John Jones, of Windsor, says it's the best and the smartest British sportster ever produced he can be sure of a good show of approving hands from our 90 reporters.

WE LIKE . . .

Easy-to-operate centre stand
Twin carbs
Unburstable engine
Hinged dual-seat to hide tools, battery and oil-tank filler
The looks on the faces of other " sports " machine riders as I show them my exhausts (Colin Wheeler)

WE DISLIKE . . .

Position of the headlamp and ignition switches under the rider's leg. However, no one seems to want to see them spoiling the chromed headlamp shell
Abbreviated back mud-guard: the pillion passenger gets sprayed with water
Petrol and oil tanks that dribble

"MOTOR CYCLE TEST"

MEAN MAXIMUM SPEEDS: Bottom, *53 mph; second- *70 mph; third, 96 mph; top, 110 mph. *Valve float occurring.
HIGHEST ONE-WAY SPEED: 112 mph (conditions: damp track, light tail wind. Rider wearing one-piece leathers).
MEAN SPEED at end of quarter-mile from rest: 94 mph.
MEAN TIME to cover standing quarter-mile: 14.6s.
PETROL CONSUMPTION: At 30 mph, 100 mpg; at 40 mph, 88 mpg; at 50 mph, 78 mpg; at 60 mph, 66 mpg; at 70 mph, 54 mpg.
BRAKING: From 30 mph to rest on dry asphalt: 30ft 6in.

NORTON and BSA

NEXT? Well, the Norton Jubilee report is on the stocks at the moment—so don't delay sending in your contribution.

After the Jubilee we'll be dealing with the big BSAs—A65 and A50 twins. The models were introduced in January, 1962, so there are enough around by now. But, please, no A65Rs or Lightnings.

If you don't feel like writing at length, just drop us a postcard and we will send you a questionnaire to complete—this is the form that all contributors fill in eventually.

When writing your report try to group your ideas under headings such as the ones in this Bonneville report—handling, performance, electrics and so forth.

Address your contributions to either Jubilee or BSA Riders' Reports, Motor Cycle, Dorset House, Stamford Street, London, SE1.

649 cc TRIUMPH Thunderbird

ROAD TESTS OF NEW MODELS

WHY NOT ask a policeman? If you want to know what makes a Thunderbird tick you can't go far wrong there. Despite the fact that police models are now somewhat sanctified, there is enough T-bird in evidence to tell you that this is a machine with an enviable reputation. It is a direct descendant of the legendary pre-war Speed Twin and, in its new unit-construction guise, it must surely be the peppiest and smoothest of all.

The 6T is the machine for gobbling up the miles. Delightfully comfortable, with that peculiar but effective Triumph swept-back handlebar, and with a surprisingly high top speed, in the region of 100 mph, the Thunderbird is ideal for long-distance touring.

No frills, no twin carbs, yet this machine with a competent rider at the helm will show off the sporty boys with their clip-ons and rear-sets on any long trip. You just don't need to stop so often to recuperate!

When first taken over for test, the 6T suffered from abnormal vibration throughout the range. A cracked main bearing was diagnosed by the factory although, in fact, nothing appeared to be wrong when the engine was stripped.

After careful reassembly the power unit was infinitely sweeter and what vibration there was was confined to the range above 80 mph. Even then it was not annoying.

The test machine was not new. It had had a very hard life on the factory test strength and, despite its mere 3,000 miles, gave the appearance of being older.

That is why not too much store was placed by the occasional rust spot and blemish on the paintwork. The chrome appeared to be of good quality and remained in perfect condition.

Half-an-hour with the polish can and a rag brought back the sort of finish we expect from a Triumph. Especially commendable is the extremely clean and compact engine unit which remained completely free from extraneous oil throughout the 2,000 miles of the test.

Looking back on those miles, there is one aspect of the Thunderbird which stands out of the host of good points.

Left: Comfort is the Thunderbird keynote; it can be gunned for hours without fatigue.
Below: The general lines are functional and very clean. Absence of rear panelling gives the machine a businesslike air.
Above: Engine and gear box are built as one. The petrol tank holds four gallons

It is the readiness with which the engine starts. Although it was not possible to test starting in really cold weather, the 6T invariably started first kick during the test.

The air lever, if necessary at all, could be opened immediately without distress from the engine. Even from cold the machine would tick over reliably.

With plenty of beefy power on tap, and the sort of acceleration usually associated with a sports bike, the Thunderbird is at home under any conditions.

It will trickle along in traffic, or howl around the MIRA test track at over 90 mph—and all the time it gives the impression that it is built specially for the job in hand, whatever it may be.

Although this isn't the machine on which you need to use the gear box if you want to get places, it is great fun to ride if you do wish to play a concerto on the box. Gear changing—especially selecting bottom from rest—had been crunchy before the engine was stripped.

But the subsequent readjustment of the clutch during assembly cured all the trouble. The change was then light and precise; clutch action could not be faulted, even after a long series of searing standing starts during the acceleration test figures.

Triumphs in the past have had a reputation, unwarranted in the eyes of many, for be-

low-par handling. Yet on this latest Thunderbird there is no trace of the erstwhile whip at high speeds.

The bike can be confidently cranked into 70-mph bends without any sign of bother. If the throttle is eased, or the brakes are gently applied, in the course of negotiating a fast bend the back of the machine will waddle a little.

This is predictable with most two-wheelers, and was never serious enough to cause concern.

Just as the Thunderbird is ideal for long distances because of its thrashability and armchair comfort, it is distinctly outstanding for its economy.

There can be few machines of this capacity and performance which will return a genuine overall consumption of 60

mpg—with 70 mph cruising wherever possible.

The latest Lucas 12-volt electrics make night riding a pleasure. The penetrating, powerful headlight is sufficient for cruising in the upper sixties on unlit roads. Higher speeds would probably be possible, if not illegal.

Show the Triumph an open road and it is content to cruise all day at seventy. Experience at MIRA proved that a speed between 80 and 90 mph is well within the sustained capabilities of the machine.

Braking from these speeds is controlled and more than satisfactory. The powerful brakes bring the bike to rest in the minimum distance with no fuss or alarm whatsoever.

The Triumph Thunderbird is a machine with a long tradition; a tradition that is not

Left: Almost a Triumph trade-mark, the patented nacelle gives a pleasant aspect to the instruments. The tank-top luggage grid is very useful —another well established Triumph feature. Top: The willing power plant remained free from oil seepage throughout the test. Routine maintenance points, such as contact breaker and rockers, are readily accessible. Right: There is an accessible finger adjuster for the rear brake

In its silver and black livery, the Thunderbird is very smart and easy to clean. Wherever it goes it catches the eye

Motor Cycle Road Test

TRIUMPH THUNDERBIRD

ENGINE:
Capacity and type: 649 cc (71 x 82mm) overhead-valve parallel twin.
Bearings: Two ball mains; plain big ends.
Lubrication: Dry sump; capacity 5 pints.
Compression ratio: 7.5 to 1.
Carburettor: Amal Monobloc with dry-felt air filter. Air slide operated by handlebar lever.
Claimed output: 37 bhp at 6,700 rpm.

TRANSMISSION:
Primary: ⅜in duplex chain in oilbath case.
Secondary: ⅝ x ⅜in chain.
Clutch: Multi-plate running in oil.
Gear ratios: 11.43; 7.77; 5.47; 4.6 to 1.
Engine rpm at 30 mph in top gear: 1,850.

ELECTRICAL EQUIPMENT:
Ignition: Battery and twin coils; 12 volt.
Charging: Lucas 100-watt alternator to two six-volt, 8-amp-hour batteries through rectifier.
Headlamp: 7in diameter with 50/40-watt main bulb.

FUEL CAPACITY: 4 gallons.

TYRES: Dunlop 3.25 x 18in ribbed front; 3.50 x 18in studded rear.

BRAKES: 8in diameter front, 7in diameter rear, both with floating shoes; finger adjusters.

SUSPENSION: Triumph telescopic front fork with hydraulic damping. Pivoted rear fork controlled by Girling spring-and-hydraulic units; three-position adjustment for load.

DIMENSIONS: Wheelbase, 55in. Ground clearance, 5in. Seat height, 30in. All unladen.

WEIGHT: 377 lb, fully equipped, with full oil tank and approximately one gallon of petrol.
PRICE: £308 3s, including British purchase tax.
ROAD TAX: £8 a year; £2 19s for four months.
MAKERS: Triumph Engineering Co, Ltd, Meriden Works, Allesley, Coventry, Warwickshire.

PERFORMANCE

PERFORMANCE:
(Obtained at the Motor Industry Research Association's Proving Ground, Lindley, Leicestershire.)
HIGHEST ONE-WAY SPEED: 101 mph (10½-stone rider wearing one-piece leathers; moderate following wind).
BRAKING: From 30 mph to rest on dry tarmac, 29ft.
TURNING CIRCLE: 18ft.
MINIMUM NON-SNATCH SPEED: 18 mph in top gear
WEIGHT PER CC: 0.58 lb.

Access to the tool roll, batteries and oil-tank cap is gained by hinging the dualseat to the left

belied by the 1966 model. Along with your generous helping of performance, smoothness and comfort, you get refinements like the tank-top luggage grid, that neat nacelle, and the extremely convenient hinged dualseat for access to the oil tank and batteries.

Only the plastic tool tray under the seat lets the side down. · It is too small to accommodate the tool kit without a great deal of careful fiddling and packing, and the one on the test machine soon disintegrated through overloading.

Although more than average effort is necessary to haul the bike on to the roll-on stand, the 6T remains a handleable, compact machine that no one would have difficulty in manoeuvring.

If you want a machine that is supremely capable under all conditions, a machine to give sports bike performance without the trimmings, a machine to take you and a passenger effortlessly over mile after mile, then the smart '66 T-Bird is definitely your cup of tea. And there's plenty of sugar in that thar char'

BOTTOM   **SECOND**    **THIRD**   **TOP**

Bottom-, second- and third-gear figures represent maximum-power revs, 6,700 rpm

ACCELERATION

STANDING QUARTER-MILE: Terminal speed, 86 mph Time, 15.6s

FUEL CONSUMPTION

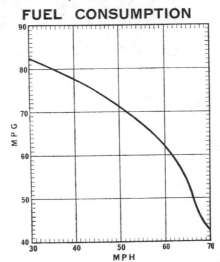

ROAD TESTS OF NEW MODELS

490 cc TRIUMPH Tiger 100

ALTHOUGH the very first Tiger 100 model was introduced long before many of us even saw the light of day—1939, to be precise—continuous development over the years has ensured that this 100-mph twin has kept its place in the popularity poll. Records of the ISDT show its successes in the past—and, this year, the power unit of every machine in our Trophy Team is, basically, the Tiger 100 engine.

What is the secret of this long-standing attraction? The latest Meriden model provides the answer quite simply; performance aplenty with the minimum of fuss. Once, if you had a bike with a three-figure maximum, you didn't quibble too much about fussiness and lack of tractability at the bottom of the rev-range.

But this Triumph, with its straightforward, single-carburettor specification, will hold its own in the fiercest of company. And if you roll back the grip, another side of its character immediately appears.

The Tiger will pad along at 30 mph in top in a way that won't attract a second glance. Come to a standstill at traffic lights and idling, at just under 1,000 rpm, continues without hesitation until you are ready to go.

For getting places fast, this extremely peppy 490 cc engine will hoist you from a standstill to the 70-mph legal maximum in a paltry ten seconds. And the power arrives progressively.

Often enough, five-hundred roadsters have been made to top the magic ton by using cams which give the valve gear a very hard life and compression ratios which demand top-octane brews.

Power will be virtually non-existent until halfway through

tion for overtaking. All this on premium-grade fuel.

The Tiger 100 is quite capable of cruising at 70 mph indefinitely. Indeed, at the MIRA test track it proved well able to keep up an 85-mph gait without tiring.

In common with all the other twins in the range, this model has 12-volt electrics as standard. Lights were adequate for after-dark riding up to the legal limit. Both the speedometer (which read 6-mph fast throughout) and revmeter are lit and easily seen.

The light switch is mounted on the left-side panel below the seat nose. This position is inconvenient. It would be an improvement to locate it in the headlamp shell.

The ignition switch is mounted on the same panel, but the shortcoming of not being able to reach it quickly is offset by the provision of a cut-out button on the right side of the handlebar.

Triumph electrical equipment includes a 35-amp fuse in a plastic capsule under the

seat. This proved useful during the test when a faulty stop-light switch caused a short-circuit.

A machine which is difficult to start is a nuisance. In this respect the Tiger 100 earned full marks, for rarely did it need more than a second prod, hot or cold.

The air slide is operated by a spring-loaded plunger on top of the carburettor. This on-off arrangement, while effective, is a little awkward for, ideally, a gradual opening of the slide is needed.

CLICK

Gear engagement from rest is often criticized on Triumphs. On the test model, a slight click was the worst noise experienced.

Clutch operation was excellent—really light in action, progressive and positive in taking up the drive, but the clutch (and front-brake) handlebar lever needed a greater-than-average hand span to operate it comfortably.

Worthy of mention is that gears can be changed as swiftly as the pedal can be moved. Pedal action was so light that it seemed there was nothing connected to it!

Riding position is comfortable for those of average build, but a six-foot staffman could have done with a little more leg room.

Suspension, front and rear, was a little on the firm side but this helped to provide predictable handling when flicking the model through corners at speeds up to the present legal limit. Of course, the all-up weight of under 350 lb helps to make this model an ideal bend-swinging device.

In all normal angles of lean grounding is never a worry; both stands and the silencers are well clear.

Brakes were right up to standard; they gave smooth, powerful deceleration at all speeds.

For 1966 the oil-tank size was upped by a pint to six pints. A rear-chain oiler is

Pride and joy of any enthusiast's heart, the Tiger 100 positively radiates competition ancestry

the rev-range—then it comes in with a rush.

But on the test model there is a smooth spread of power up to the peak, 7,000 rpm. For absolutely maximum performance, gear changes should certainly be left until the revmeter needle swings round to this mark, but for ordinary fast road use, gears can be swopped around 5,000 rpm.

It is not necessary to play tunes on the gear box to keep up the pace. A drop into third provides brisk accelera-

The twin contact-breakers neatly set in the timing-chest cover. Just two screws need be undone to free the plate

The 490 cc power unit. It remained oil-tight for the period of the test

alone a puncture outfit, is too small.

A word of praise for the tank-top carrying grid; this is a familiar but extremely welcome feature.

A redesigned tank motif makes the name stand out boldly and, if you value being exclusive, this Tiger 100 is the first Triumph to sport a green finish.

If you are looking for a machine with an ancestry that will stamp you as a discerning rider, give you performance plus fun when riding, take a passenger if you wish and leave your budget in a reasonably healthy state as well, it's time you talked Tiger 100 with your Triumph dealer.

Below: The 35-amp main fuse in the battery lead. This saves wiring and components in case of a short-circuit

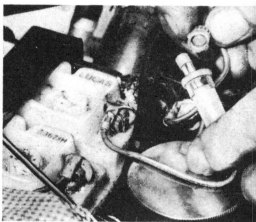

supplied from the return side of the lubrication system but, on the test model, this seemed reluctant to work properly.

The power unit remained commendably oil-tight except for a weep round the gearbox filler plug. Just a pint of oil was needed to top up the tank each 600 miles.

Cruising for long distances at 70 mph (a shade over 5,000 rpm) made one aware of high-frequency vibration through handlebar and footrests. On short trips this was not too annoying.

Accessibility for routine maintenance is first class. Carburettor, air filter, rockers and contact-breaker can all be reached easily. Both brakes have finger adjusters. The Triumph feature of a side-hinged dualseat makes checking the oil level and topping-up the battery a few moments' work.

On the debit side, the space provided to keep tools, let

Smartly finished in green, cream and black, the Triumph is set off by a chromium-plated headlamp shell

ACCELERATION

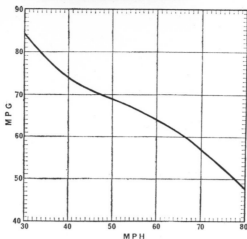

STANDING QUARTER-MILE:
Terminal speed, 85 mph
Time, 15.2s

FUEL CONSUMPTION

BOTTOM

SECOND

THIRD

TOP

Bottom-, second- and third-gear figures represent maximum power revs, 7,000

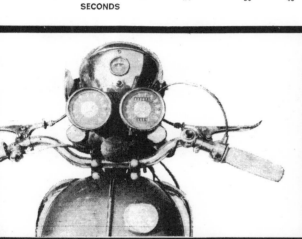

Above: Symmetrical revmeter-speedometer layout. Above right: Carburettor with its dry felt air filter and plunger-operated air slide

Motor Cycle ROAD TESTS

SPECIFICATION

ENGINE
Capacity and type: 490 cc (69 × 65.5mm) parallel twin with pushrod operated valves.
Bearings: Ball drive-side and plain timing-side mains; plain big-ends.
Lubrication: Dry sump; tank capacity, six pints.
Compression ratio: 9 to 1.
Carburettor: Amal Monobloc with dry-felt air filter. Air slide operated by spring-loaded plunger on carburettor. Claimed output: 34 bhp at 7,000 rpm.

TRANSMISSION
Primary: ⅜in duplex chain in oilbath case.
Secondary: ⅝ × ⅜in chain.
Clutch: Multi-plate running in oil.
Gear ratios: 13.8, 9.3, 6.7 and 5.7 to 1.
Engine rpm at 30 mph in top gear: 2,270.

ELECTRICAL EQUIPMENT
Ignition: Battery and twin coils.
Charging: Lucas 100-watt alternator to two six-volt, eight-amp-hour batteries through rectifier. (One 12-volt, 10-amp-hour battery being fitted to current production models.)
Headlamp: 7in diameter with 50/40-watt main bulb.

FUEL CAPACITY: 3 gallons
TYRES: Dunlop 3.25 × 18in ribbed front; 3.50 × 18in studded rear.
BRAKES: 7in diameter front and rear, both with floating shoes; finger adjusters.

SUSPENSION: Triumph telescopic front fork with hydraulic damping. Pivoted rear fork controlled by Girling spring-and-hydraulic units; three-position adjustment for load.
DIMENSIONS: Wheelbase, 55in; ground clearance, 6in; seat height, 30in. All unladen.
WEIGHT: 340 lb, fully equipped, with full oil tank and approximately one gallon of petrol.
PRICE: £296 3s 5d, including British purchase tax.
ROAD TAX: £8 a year; £2 19s for four months.
MAKERS: Triumph Engineering Co, Ltd, Meriden Works, Allesley, Coventry, Warwickshire.

PERFORMANCE

(Obtained at the Motor Industry Research Association's Proving Ground, Lindley, Leicestershire.)
MEAN MAXIMUM SPEED: 97 mph (11½-stone rider wearing two-piece riding suit; moderate following wind.)
HIGHEST ONE-WAY SPEED: 100 mph.
BRAKING: From 30 mph to rest on dry tarmac, 31ft.
TURNING CIRCLE: 14 ft 6in.
MINIMUM NON-SNATCH SPEED: 18 mph in top gear.
WEIGHT PER CC: 0.69 lb